True to the End

A Journey Into the Burdens and Risks of Executorship

GERMAINE DECHANT

 FriesenPress

Suite 300 - 990 Fort St
Victoria, BC, V8V 3K2
Canada

www.friesenpress.com

Back cover photo: Darcy Finley Photography

ISBN
978-1-03-910694-9 (Hardcover)
978-1-03-910693-2 (Paperback)
978-1-03-910695-6 (eBook)

1. Biography & Autobiography, Personal Memoirs

Distributed to the trade by The Ingram Book Company

Table of Contents

In memory of

Marilyn

With love and gratitude

for the gift of a remarkable friendship

50 years strong

"If anyone offers you an amazing opportunity
and you're not sure you can do it, say yes,
then learn how to do it."

—Richard Branson

1

—

Disaster Strikes Twice

"Marilyn is sound asleep right now and, sadly, she won't be with us much longer." This was Elena's opening after the briefest exchange of pleasantries. I gave her points for being direct. Elena could be the heart of compassion and kindness personified. She could also be blunt or diplomatic, depending on the circumstances, but either way she knew how to get her message across with unapologetic frankness. She had never been one to beat around the bush.

"I'm going to be straight with you," she said.

I hesitated, fear sliding up my spine at her words, at the firm and solemn tone of her voice, a hint of steel beneath it as if she were bracing her own self for what she had to say. The simple fact that she was the one who had answered the phone put me on high alert.

"Okay. What's going on?" I asked, managing to keep my voice steady.

She knew I needed to know, so she gave me the lowdown on what was happening with Marilyn.

"She stopped eating and drinking two days ago. She can no longer walk; she sleeps most of the day, is barely communicative and needs complete care."

Darkness can take many forms in our lives and, as you can imagine, it's hard to hear that your friend is dying. I felt her words like a solid smack on the chin, sharp and brutal.

"How can that be, Elena? She was still driving, shopping for groceries, and enjoying your visit when I talked with her two weeks ago."

"I know it's hard to believe—even for me, and I see her every day. She's showing a shockingly rapid decline. You'd better come soon if you want a chance to say goodbye."

I felt my heart shatter at the news coming to me from what felt like a bolt right out of the blue that rattled my sense of stability. Curled up in my favourite chair with a glass of fragrant Okanagan Riesling in hand, I hadn't expected to pick up the phone to such hard news. I'd anticipated a long chat with my dear friend, Marilyn. We hadn't seen each other for two years. What we lacked in proximity we made up for with long-distance conversations, scheduled without fail, every second Monday. Getting old and living alone in poor health is a perfect formula for loneliness. I knew she had grown profoundly lonely over the last few years, and I had reflected with her on the powerful relationship between longing for health, aliveness, independence, and the loneliness she struggled with. Our visits often included detailed discussions of her out-of-control medical conditions and updates on the medical interventions planned or in place to deal with these physical betrayals. We debated the pluses and minuses of one treatment over another, all things that would never have entered our thoughts a few years ago. We also focused beyond the painful issues on the positives in our lives. We often laughed out loud at private jokes and silly things, the most recent of which was a comment Marilyn had overheard while grocery shopping. Someone had said:

"A red-headed gal in a beautiful new dress is proof that God's a man."

To appreciate why this really grabbed her attention, you have to know that Marilyn was a redhead and, yes, with the fiery temper redheads are noted for.

* * *

"With Home Care services in place, she's getting what she needs to be comfortable right now, but we're working on having her placed in hospice care before we leave tomorrow."

Elena and her husband, Patrick, Marilyn's closest friends and my friends for many years, had been with Marilyn for a full month, devoted to supporting her in every possible way.

"Can you stay a few more days, Elena? Until I get there?"

"No. We've been away a long time now and really need to get home."

Processing as we talked, I realized I shouldn't feel so dumb-struck, having seen the oncology report Marilyn emailed me after one of our recent conversations. The report, now four months old, described extensive tumour growth in her kidneys and bladder with widespread metastasis to her bones and lymph nodes. It con-cluded with a projected life expectancy of six months. She was frail at the age of 78, and I now admitted to myself that she had been dying for months with multiple comorbidities, crippling pain, and the intrusive treatments eating up her days.

I have profound death anxiety that borders on phobia and a tendency for magical thinking when it comes to my loved ones—it won't happen if I don't acknowledge it. I have trouble letting go and have never learned how to get better at it, so avoiding death thoughts whenever possible makes sense to me. I was ashamed to realize that my mind had chosen to deny her reality so blatantly staring me in the face. Perhaps ignorance is bliss, but in this case, the result of my denial was that I probably hadn't given her the support she needed. I would have to find a way to make up for that somehow. Over the last few years, she had experienced a series of health crises for which the medical interventions could only offer brief and temporary rescue.

"It's one damn thing after another with few breaks in between!" she'd say in her frustration. I now understood Marilyn's refusal of nourishment as a bold statement of her choice to end the pain. It's not that her number was up necessarily, to use Marilyn's own favourite expression. But the cruelty of her illness had stripped away all elements of well-being, robbing her of any potential for quality of life. She was done with this life, and while I perceived death as the ultimate enemy sneaking in, and I would rage mightily against the dying of the light, she was accepting the wisdom of Ecclesiastes—there is a time to love and a time to die—and was welcoming death as her invited guest.

I believed she had decided that enough was enough; a person can only bear so much. Refusing food and drink was her way of saying: "I'm ready and I'll do it my way." She was ready to confront the realities of her diseased body. I was not. It was that simple—and that complicated. I might wish that she'd chosen at the very least to sip fine Okanagan wine on her way out and that she hadn't given up. But for a person in intractable pain, dying may not be a tragedy. If she decided it was time, it was time. Still, death is a mess, I thought. It's expensive. It's disruptive. It gets in the way of everyone's plans. And then guilt sat on my chest and squeezed my gut for thinking any and all of that, and I longed to do what felt like the most important thing I could possibly be doing—to drop everything and rush to her side, to hold her hand so she wouldn't feel alone in this final journey.

"You know how stubborn she can be. She's resisting going to hospice care," continued Elena, interrupting my distressed processing. "I've arranged for her doctor to come by later today. Marilyn trusts her and will listen."

Her doctor was convincing. That evening, Marilyn was placed in the local hospice.

* * *

I believe arriving at a degree of acceptance on our mortality is a process, not an epiphany. I also believe it takes courage to ponder deeply our own mortality and to take the necessary steps to prepare for it. Such courage is difficult, but Marilyn didn't shrink from it. She acknowledged that as her time drew near, the responsibility for decisions would shift away from her. I admired how well she had prepared herself for this eventuality, as I believe we all should. She had taken her end-of-life decisions seriously and put all the right things in place. It was evident that she had received very good legal advice in the process and had understood the options and the need for action. Her affairs were in order.

In her Representation Agreement, she had appointed her life-long friend Elena as her Personal Care Representative, clearly outlining Elena's authority, responsibilities, and limitations in the health and personal care decisions Marilyn would need help with or could no longer make for herself. This could include important decisions beyond health and medical procedures, such as living arrangements—which would include organizing hospice care—personal needs, and end-of-life care. There was no doubt that she trusted Elena to accept the responsibility and act honestly and in good faith on her behalf. Marilyn knew that Elena shared her values and would follow her wishes in choosing the least intrusive course of action appropriate for her. She had also included what is commonly known as a "living will"—her wishes about her end-of-life care, a statement that would prove immensely helpful during a difficult and emotional time.

Marilyn had also signed an Enduring Power of Attorney document, appointing Patrick as her Attorney. Many people believe that to be designated an Attorney, you have to be a lawyer, but that's not the case. Anyone of legal age can serve in this capacity. The document, effective immediately upon being signed and in effect up to the time of her death, authorized Patrick to act on her behalf with respect to her property and financial affairs. He would hold the same powers as she did in regards to day-to-day tasks ranging from opening her mail, paying her bills, banking, and even looking after her pets to the more complex work of filing her tax returns, dealing with her accountants and lawyers, and potentially even voting on her behalf. He would also keep meticulous accounts of all transactions. The role also comes with limitations, thankfully. Patrick would not, for example, have the right to alter Marilyn's will or grant Power of Attorney to someone else on her behalf. I thought Marilyn had made a very good choice in appointing Patrick to this role. I believed him to be naturally gifted in money matters. The Patrick I knew would act with honesty and integrity on her behalf and with the well-being of her family top-of-mind— important qualities in a role that comes with tremendous power and responsibilities that could be daunting, to say the least.

And in bold letters on the front page of her Last Will and Testament, you would see that Marilyn had appointed me as the Executor of her will and Trustee of her estate, entrusting me to carry out her instructions and final wishes. She hadn't appointed an alternate to serve should I not be available when the time came—either an oversight on her part or perhaps she just had great confidence in me.

She had mailed the three of us fully-executed copies of these documents after connecting us with her lawyer for the required signatures. As I think of this with the benefit of hindsight, I realize how smart she was. She could have chosen to finalize all of this under a veil of secrecy, but her approach created a team, with the three of us on the same page, understanding each other's role, and easing and accelerating all processes in her end-of-life health and business needs as well as with the management of her estate. One drawback in her appointment decisions was that not one of us lived close by. Location is important for obvious reasons, as is the ability to travel if necessary. Cleary Marilyn banked on the latter.

Elena and Patrick were now free to go. Having helped Marilyn with major health and personal care decisions, Elena had completed her role as a devoted caregiver and as Marilyn's Personal Care Representative. Patrick, with Enduring Power of Attorney, had facilitated a number of important financial transactions with Marilyn while she was still competent to make decisions but too weak physically to follow through with the required tasks. Now that Marilyn was where she needed to be, they could go home confident they had done all they could for her. With heavy hearts, they said their last goodbye and hit the road.

In a last conversation before they left, I voiced my lack of confidence in performing the role of Executor. I had a strong feeling that I should give this "opportunity" a solid NO and that I should get out of Dodge as fast as I could. In hindsight I know that it was my sorrow presenting as fear. Giving in to my rising panic, I sheepishly asked Patrick, with more hope than reason, if he'd be willing to assume this role in my place, since he was already there and was very knowledgeable about Marilyn's financials. Also, I knew he had done this work before.

I'm acutely embarrassed to admit that I tried to weasel my way out of the role.

"I come to you cup-in-hand, Patrick. All it would take to make the transfer official would be Marilyn's signature on the appropriate legal document while she's still capable."

But my entreaties fell on deaf ears.

"Not a chance," he said. "Marilyn wanted you in this role for good reason. She knew your skills. She trusted you absolutely and unconditionally to carry out her wishes after her death. I know this is a unique and demanding job, and I'll help you if you need me, but I must get home now."

"Ahhh, Patrick, Marilyn's faith in me is touching, but this needs to be a story with a happy ending. You and I both know everyone loves a happy ending. I feel ill-equipped to achieve that result."

"Relax," he said, a note of steel in his voice. "This is not a walk in the park, I know, and not a job for the fainthearted. But you'll be fine with this."

"But Patrick, I haven't done any big project work for a couple of years now. My brain is on permanent holiday. In all seriousness, and as much as I dislike acknowledging this, I don't think I have the knowledge to take this on."

"No buts. You've handled much more complicated matters in your professional roles. Besides, it's a moot point. Marilyn is no longer in a condition to sign legal documents."

I knew Patrick to be an accomplished businessman, and I had confidence in his judgement, but as much as I felt grateful for his kind words, I wasn't sure I could trust them.

I wasn't the kind of person who typically made decisions on the fly, but I had promised Marilyn I would serve as her Executor four years ago, in a moment of madness and without giving any thought to the responsibilities involved. Through my parents' teachings, my life's philosophy was to be generous and not pull away when asked for help. It felt now as if in saying yes to Marilyn's request I had agreed to being dropped into the middle of a strange land where I needed to find my way around—without a map.

I've spent most of my adult life in positions of leadership and have been many things in my journey, as the string of initials after my name certifies. After several decades of growth, of building confidence immersed in professional practice and significant career achievements, I've succeeded well beyond my wildest dreams.

In my professional world, I long ago developed strategies to control, even conceal at times, what I defined as inadequacies, to prevent me from stumbling and making a fool of myself. But in the privacy of my own mind, self-doubts were now alive and distressing. When it came to others, I was generous without fail. When it came to myself…not so much. I thought about the person everyone sees when they look at me—the competence and string of accomplishments. Yes, that's a big part of who I am. It's hard for me to talk about it, but that person is a bit afraid of this other me whose mind, I know, is also notorious as an instrument of self-torture. As the evil critic in my head, the voice I can never ignore, insisted that I was inadequate for this role, I wondered how I could even get started. What was I thinking? Serving as Executor had, after all, not been part of my life's plan—probably not what I was born to do, not a long-held professional dream, not a match with anything I had prepared for, and certainly not an item on my bucket list. Now that the task was in front of me, I was full of apprehension and, despite Patrick's encouragement, feeling that I didn't even know where to begin.

As if the great sorrow generated by Marilyn's impending death wasn't enough to cope with, my entire body was flooded with a whole new set of anxieties. Partially driving this anxiety was the timing and the complexities of completing Executor work from a great distance. The literature advises against appointing an Executor who lives far away, and there are good reasons for this—the logistics of travel to get the work done, and the fact that wills and estate legislation is provincial. This imposes an additional set of information about which the Executor needs to be knowledge-able. I lived in Alberta when I signed up for this role. Now I was three provinces away.

My husband, Bill, and I moved to Winnipeg in the spring of 2016 after having lived our lives in Alberta. We spent twenty-five years in the best city in the world: St. Albert, Alberta. I'm happy to tell you I love Winnipeg, the city that Canadians love to hate. It's rare to hear a kind word about Winterpeg Mani-Snow-Ba, even though it recently cracked the top 10 on the *Lonely Planet* list of best places in the world to visit. Yes, it's been ranked higher than Vancouver and Toronto. The Peg, as locals affectionately call their city, was the only Canadian city to make the *National Geographic Traveler's Best Trips* in 2016.

Some of our family and friends were genuinely shocked when they learned we were moving here, and some even started a pool, betting on how long we'd last in this winter city. We found out that the longest guess was one year. One winter would make the decision abundantly obvious, they figured. Now that's confidence for you! One of the farewell gifts I received was a heavy black wool scarf with a matching tuque with an Alberta company logo emblazoned in bright red letters across the front. We didn't take offense at the teasing. We rolled with the jokes, happily joining in the fun. It's important to laugh at yourself, after all. We still get teased about being Winterpeggers. My friend Shain says, "You have to say it correctly—it's Winterpeg, Man-its -colda." No need to feel sorry for us, friends. Although we miss you in so many ways and will always identify with Albertans at heart, we're happy here and wouldn't have it any other way—except for one thing. Stick with me, I'll tell you what that is in a moment.

So why Winnipeg? It can't be the weather, that's for sure. January and February offer days of slap-in-your-face 40 below windy weather. I'll be the first to tell you I'm not a winter warrior. What I've learned, though, is that most Winnipegers (and Albertans, for that matter) are on surprisingly good terms with winter. You'll hear my brother, Fern, say things like this with a laugh, dismissing the bitter cold: "Guess what, the cold spell has broken. It's only -26 here this morning. Come on down and enjoy our chinook."

Could it be the case that we in the Prairies excel at denial?

Are we happy here because of the city's proximity to the lakes? No. That only means many hot, humid summer days that are quite unbearable—to me, at least. Long-term Winterpegers just go to the lake every chance they get. In fact, the city seems to empty out every weekend. Weekends are the best time to go shopping, as the malls are pretty empty.

Can it be because it's the home of the Winnipeg Jets? Go, Jets, Go! Bill has become an enthusiastic fan. My favourite part is the singing of the national anthem. After that, I leave the room, but he keeps me up to date on the wins and losses.

Can it be because of its 150-year history as the economic hub for agriculture in the prairies? This actually resonates for us because of our family farm history.

Surprise! None of the above.

Winnipeg is indeed a city of well-kept secrets, but we love it for one reason only: our daughter, Kristianne, lives here with her husband, Jamie, and two little boys, Zachary and Noah. And that was the reason for our move here—to spend our retirement years immersed in the lives of our grandsons. Having grown up on the farm as the children of pioneers—Bill with seven siblings and me with eight brothers and four sisters— we are hardwired for family and work as our top priorities. Can you imagine my mother making breakfast, lunch, and dinner for a family of fifteen day in and day out without fail? There was no takeout or Skip the Dishes in those days. Like her, family and devotion are the focus that make our lives whole, rich, safe, and stable. Everything else is incidental. Here, close to our grandsons, we know we can make a significant contribution while selfishly harvesting one of life's simple joys—precious time spent with our little boys.

Moving here wasn't an easy decision, because our son, Anthony, and his wife, Karmon, and our precious granddaughter, Elise, live in Calgary, Alberta. They are far away in miles but next-door neighbours in our hearts. Seeing them only four or five times a year on family visits is never enough, and departures always trigger tears in all of us. File that under heartache! So that's what I'd like to change. I would love for our son's family to be right next door or for us to be in two places at once. Then our world would be perfect. In the meantime, we are profoundly grateful for the marvellous technology that allows frequent FaceTime and makes living provinces away less far away than it used to be. But we don't deceive ourselves; it is not the same as real time together.

Our life, as you can appreciate, has changed in dramatic ways since our retirement and move to the Peg. Before moving, we bought a 35-year-old house two blocks from our daughter's family home in one of the city's prestigious central neighbourhoods and within a short drive to more comprehensive amenities and services than we'll ever need. In fact, I can't think of a single thing missing in this neighbourhood. Best of all is a six-minute drive to the local library. I am a creature of books and have been since I was old enough to hold one in my hands. I could tell you stories about my frustration as a child at having read all the books in my little country school library by the time I reached grade four. As a shameless lifelong student and certified nerd, I love libraries and am deeply grateful for their services, a great gift to our communities.

Our choice of location was very intentional. Having commuted several kilometres in hellish traffic all the years of my career, I was resolved to live just a short walk from my grandchildren. We moved into a run-down house that had been vacant for five years. This is where we decided we would sink our roots in Winnipeg. The house needed more than tender loving care. It needed a complete make-over. It had good bones and a strong foundation built to last but, I'm sad to report, no ghosts. It opened its arms to us in welcome as we took it apart and brought it back to life, beautifully modernized for function, convenience, and comfort. My husband, Bill, especially enjoyed this project, given his engineering background and well-honed handyman skills. For years we and many of our friends called him Mister Fixit while keeping a honey-do list for him that never seemed to disappear. We fully subscribed to the belief: "A handyman's work is never done." Bill also liked the yard work, which was great because there was a lot of landscaping to do.

Living in our home while it was undergoing extensive renovation was interesting, fun, and chaotic. I loved the workers and developed a special friendship with Rob, who supervised most of the projects. I teased him about the indispensable leather tool-belt slung at his hips, knowing that if I had to carry that load, I'd quickly collapse. His were not the hands of an amateur.

"This isn't my first rodeo," he'd say with a grin and a nod when presented with a problem. He'd mull over the options and then bring forward a solution to any problem. The buzz of activity was music to my ears and every completed piece was a WOW! But I won't lie to you—living in a construction zone was hard work and very stressful. The constant dust and mess everywhere was enough to drive me to drink. A frequent source of hilarity during the process was my grandson, Zachary, who was four at the time. He'd pause with each visit as he came in the front door and ask for a cloth to help clean the dust.

"Don't worry," he'd say without fail and with great emphasis, "we'll get this job done!"

A highlight for me was the two full days a week I spent looking after Noah, who had just turned one, at his home—away from the noise and disorder of construction. I also enjoyed my inspection of the progress at my house at the end of each day. Bill loved going AWOL at least once a week. None of us knew where he went, but it had to be a haven for a Bill-of-all-trades, since he always returned thrilled with his exotic loot of some kind of specialized tool and little brown bags full of various bits of shiny hardware.

Apart from a few minor caveats, the contractors we hired did exceptionally high-quality work, and we felt so lucky to finish the project, at least the major parts of it, after nine months of hard work by early November, when it became too cold to work from the garage. The tools were put away for the winter. Ahhh, blessed relief! A beautiful house and winter months by the fireplace to plan the remaining project details to be continued in the spring.

Our life took on a quiet rhythm, free after 30 years as a driven Health Care Executive on call around the clock, burning buckets of midnight oil, thriving on always having something new to learn. I was disciplined, achieving, growing, and ascending, and I would have bristled if anyone suggested I was not on my game. I now appreciated my role as a grandmother and held my time nurturing a relationship with my three grandchildren as sacred, the very heart of life, days of exquisite non-productivity in which I could completely escape in the timeless magic of their child's world. I loved the exhilarating freedom of my days and the wholesome pace of my retirement—a pace that said almost everything could wait until tomorrow, especially if there was a good book around. And guess what—there always was an ample supply stacked and shelved for ease of access here and there in every corner of the house. Lost in those pages, I lived in a world of storybook privilege and in such a constant discovery mode, I relished the excitement of never having to live the same day twice. I was otherwise busy enough with my volunteer governance work on the board of an international development agency, my two days a week with Noah plus frequent family visits, and the relentless work of homemaking. Everything about my days was an amazing gift. Weeks without beginning or end, far from the hustle-bustle of a demanding work life. Every day a Sunday. I counted my blessings and wasn't looking for new challenges. Neither was Bill, who was also enjoying his free time, happy to have left behind his executive life. Our comfort and contentment with life was at a high point, and we considered ourselves incredibly fortunate.

Until one day, six months after our house renovations were completed, life threw us a nasty curveball. Disaster struck, bringing home the truth that even with the best laid plans, no condition lasts forever. Our lives changed dramatically.

As winter progressed, what had started for Bill as mild back discomfort became unbearable back pain, advancing daily to the point where he could barely walk.

"You can hug me," he'd say, "but not too hard."

Despite noble efforts, medical intervention failed to provide a single helpful solution. Then on a memorable Friday, May 19, 2017, his back broke. Literally. And we were propelled into crisis mode. I begged to be allowed to ride in the ambulance with him but to no avail. I stood in the open front doorway feeling uncharacteristically impotent as I watched them take my husband away. *God help us*, I prayed, to keep the fear at bay. I then wandered the house aimlessly for a few minutes, pondering my next steps. He had developed a rare condition, seen only in one in a million people, called cauda equina. I know, you've never heard of it. I hadn't either. Most people haven't. It's a highbrow Latin expression that means "horse's tail" plain and simple. It refers to the bundle of nerves at the base of the spine that is crushed, and in a worst-case scenario, severed, by broken spinal disks. It's always an emergency situation. Bill was rushed to surgery from which he emerged paralyzed from the waist down.

I'm not proud to tell you that during that first year of our Winnipeg life, I'd never driven anywhere. I walked a lot in pursuit of my goal of 10,000 steps a day, and Bill drove everywhere we went together. I remember the feeling of exhilaration years ago when I first got my driver's license. That license represented freedom and fun. After years of commuting, however, I developed a different relationship with driving. It was no longer a joy but a simple means of winding my way in heavy traffic from point A to point B. I'll admit that I became a reluctant and timid driver, with my definition of wealth being having a chauffeur. I felt lucky to have such a wonderful one. He even drove me to my hairdresser. His sudden hospitalization, however, served as a rude awakening for me. While having a chauffeur had been so seductive, it came with a heavy price: my independence. I didn't know my way around the city beyond my immediate neighbourhood. I'd been aware of this growing dependence before but hadn't been motivated to confront it. I suddenly felt panicked, and frankly, quite the saddle goose.

I called a taxi.

"My husband has been taken by ambulance to the Health Sciences Centre," I said. "Please take me there as fast as you can."

"No worries," the driver replied with an air of confidence I found reassuring. "I'll have you there in twelve minutes."

He dodged traffic, zipped around corners to all the short cuts, and somehow just made all the green lights. I think he might have even buzzed through one or two reds. I hazarded a glance at the speedometer a couple times as we headed down Waverly and then Taylor. He was going a steady ten kilometres above the speed limit. Never mind, I didn't want him to slow down. Not a word was spoken between us. He kept his eyes steady on the road as he drove. True to his word, he had us there in no time flat. I was so grateful I could have kissed him, but he was very likely much happier with the double fare I believed was the gold star he fully deserved.

How I had allowed this year to play out was haunting me. I chastised myself for having become dependent, which in the darkness of my mind equated to being incompetent. I was in a serious jam. Just the thought of driving to the city centre made me tremble. I resolved to change that and the next day, too anxious to rely entirely on my GPS, I pulled out the city map, memorized the route and then chanted it, slowly and deliberately, like a mantra, all the way to the hospital: Hennessy, Waverley, Taylor, Stafford …ending up in the William Street parkade. I told my family the street was named after Bill as a sign to let me know I was in the right place. I got there in twenty-five minutes. Of course, there was more traffic than there had been the night before! Although this drive downtown and back was initially a stressful undertaking, my daily trips to the hospital became uneventful and served as a great confidence builder for venturing out to all the other places I needed to be.

Our weekly Sunday family dinners were replaced by regular visits to the hospital. The Health Sciences Centre in downtown Winnipeg is one of the largest hospitals in Canada, with thousands of people walking its halls every day. The fact that 3,000 nurses work at the HSC gives an idea of its size. There is much to see there. Our boys, then five and two, thought of each visit as a great adventure. This was their first time in a hospital environment, yet they seemed unfazed, in fact mesmerized, by the unfamiliar picture constantly unfolding before their eyes. The line-up of police cars by the emergency department, which they could see from the upstairs hallway window, was of special interest and gave rise to endless questions. They walked up to Papa Bill's bed like it was no big deal; in fact, they were more comfortable with it than the adults, and they showed a tenderness more moving and therapeutic, I'm convinced, than Bill's pain medication.

On the first visit, when Bill was still confined to bed with paralysis from his waist to his toes, Zachary snuggled up as close to him as possible and read him a Batman book, drawing his attention to the action scenes of greatest interest as he turned the pages. Noah, known to belt out one song after another in the middle of his playschool activities and for which his teachers loved him, was glued to Papa Bill's other side. Seemingly drawing from a deep well of innate compassion and offering unconditional comfort, he sang a soft and tender rendition of "Oh, do you know the muffin man?" If there was a dry eye in that four-bed surgical bedroom that day, well, it wasn't mine.

Whereas the boys took this all in stride, I found it hard to leave him there at the mercy of dedicated professionals but strangers nonetheless, with frightening machines and procedures to face without family at his side. Who would be there to hold his hand in the darkness? Nothing left him more vulnerable than being flat on his back in a hospital bed as the male staff arrived to give him a bed bath. He hated every bit of it, ashamed of his unreliable body and distressed at being near-naked in a hospital gown. The extreme introvert who had spent his life in collared shirts and pressed slacks did not appreciate the gown with the crack in the back.

"It's OK," he mumbled. "See you tomorrow."

Three strides and I was gone, leaving the man I'd lived with for 50 years unable to help himself, alone, in his hospital bed.

Another day we enjoyed a collection of photos and watched a video of Elise's dance recital. She might as well have been in the room in person, with her smile bringing the blissful warmth and colours of a double rainbow. I saw her dance, but in my mind's eye I experienced her person with perfect clarity. Her little girl scent, a mix of floral shampoo, scented markers, cinnamon and honey. Her easy, contagious giggles. I was so grateful for the technology that brought her to us through this video, which became an important, repeated highlight in Bill's long, monotonous days, especially the days he would request no visitors. He was simply too tired.

It struck me unexpectedly and sharply as I sat at the bedside that these three children were mine—my progeny—each one a wonderful, fascinating, and overwhelming gift from a generous universe. Perfection in miniature. I cried when each one was born, filling every fibre of my being with a love beyond what any words can express. I give thanks every night for the richness they bring to my life, and I feel challenged in this role to be a good person every day, because that's the model of an elder I want to be. I want to spend as much time as possible with each of them, hoping that as they grow up, they can see me as a Grandmaman they can come to anytime for encouragement and support...or for just plain fun. The time I spend with them is integral to my happiness, and I admit freely that I feel no guilt in spoiling them.

The boys eventually took great delight in the wild rides to the cafeteria in the wheelchair, flying on Papa Bill's knees. Zachary was just the right age to try his prowess at hitching a ride on the back of the wheelchair, a novel twist on the popular spins on a Safeway shopping cart. Hold on tight and cross your fingers—it's a hospital hallway adventure. Anything could happen. Whee! Well, that was fun. Then the foot races would begin up and down the second-floor corridors, which were always empty of other outsiders. The adults would be in the visitors' alcove, each immersed in our own complicated thoughts, working to keep conversations afloat and taking turns keeping an eye on the children's happy activities. Before Bill's discharge, we saw many demonstrations from our three little children of the beautiful world our hearts know is possible. If you're from the worldview that we're all interconnected and that every act of compassion contributes to the strength of the global field of compassion, then there were many generous deposits made in those six weeks, the butterfly effects rippling out to benefit the world at large.

After six weeks of intense rehab, Bill came home. He was able to get around slowly with the use of a walker but needed a ton of support in all activities of daily living. Disability had moved in with him, taking up residence in our two-storey home and forcing us to reimagine all our daily routines. Fortunately, his spinal nerves had been crushed, not severed, but it would take time and patience for them to recover. We no longer called him Mister Fixit. We called him Man-in-a-Million. Excellent rehab treatment on an outpatient basis plus the very qualities that had made him the Reno Boss—his focus and determination—contributed to his steady improvement. By the fall, he was still needing support but was relatively independent.

2

Tuesday, November 14, 2017

—

Thy Will Be Done

This had been a big year for me. Not only had I barely settled into retirement, moved across provinces, bought a house, took it apart and rebuilt it, but I'd had to face my husband's major health crisis. The call to executorship was clearly an intrusion, and while the distance was an important issue, the fact that I had my hands full at home was an even bigger limiting factor.

Six months after his surgery, Bill still needed a lot of support. Given his condition, he certainly couldn't travel to Kelowna with me. In truth, I saw parts of me that no one else recognized. In the aftermath of his illness, his residual disability and loss of capacity, I was struggling to keep waves of grief at bay. The experience had served as a sobering lesson, leaving me with a vulnerability, an altered sense of our future, and a pervasive sense of uncertainty I had a hard time shaking. The random apprehension of loss became my steady companion.

Just because things don't go the way you plan doesn't mean they're not going the way they should, I reasoned. Perhaps this was the proverbial wake up call, not a mid-life but a retirement-life crisis, a time to shake up what might be defined as a mediocre existence with spells of agonized questions of what am I now doing with my life. Was I withering away quietly, letting myself grow old in the pattern of those who believe these should be my waning years? Had my life become fixed in a rigid pattern of daily living, parochial and without purpose, like the beautiful bookends on the shelf in front of me, currently with no books to hold? Had I reached my apogee as I entered retirement? What a limiting and dismal thought!

I mulled over these worries on my 10,000 steps in the neighbourhood park and came to a firm decision that I defined as cause for applause. No one would blame me for coasting, I'm sure, but I was not made of glass and wasn't ready to pack it all in. I would give this the green light of opportunity—weather the storm by reframing this additional challenge in my changing life circumstances into an opportunity for growth and learning rather than a hardship. Our journeys often aren't self-made but defined by others; after all, you never know what you can do until you have to.

Get going, I told myself. God hates a coward. The fact that I'm no longer a spring chicken is irrelevant. We were created for a grand adventure, and avoiding danger may be no safer in the long run than outright exposure to life's callings. Executorship might become the passport to such an adventure, opening new doors, forcing me to think new thoughts and explore new possibilities I'd never discover if I didn't say yes. It would also bring risks, but perhaps one wasn't possible without the other. Adventure calls. Time to throw caution to the wind and embrace whatever discomfort might follow. I knew this could be done with well-planned family support in place.

Despite considerable misgivings, I booked my one-way flight to leave that Friday, hoping against hope that Marilyn would hang on long enough for us to have some time together. Patrick had told me that airlines provide a discounted fare for bereaved passengers who have to make last minute travel arrangements. The policies vary across airlines, so it's important to check with each one, but they typically apply when death is imminent as well as when death has occurred. I took Patrick's advice and explained to the airline why I was flying from Winnipeg to Kelowna. I was pleasantly surprised when they gave me a bereavement discount of $55.00 plus a complementary checked bag. Go WestJet! I took this small windfall as an auspicious sign that gave me a boost of confidence. I was off to a good start.

Encouraged, I set about finding the information I needed on the role of Executor, or in my case, some would say an Executrix, the female version of Executor. I love the literal meaning of the word "execute": to carry out a plan or course of action. I chose to refer to myself as Executor, a title I understood to be without gender. I'll let you in on a secret. In addition to being a bookworm, I long ago embraced the old adage that my parents had espoused: chance favours the prepared mind. They were the first to emphasize for me that how we prepare for something highlights the building blocks of our character, sending strong messages about who we are and also influencing how others perceive us.

I was a self-declared I-don't-know-it-all with a dozen questions running through my head. It was in my nature to find the answers, but I had to remind myself that it would take time and research. I didn't have hours to spend at either the library or the bookstore, but torn between fear and curiosity, I began my search at the library with a zealot's intensity, optimistic that I would come home with arms full of reference books or, even better, I would find an Executor 101 manual for a Canadian context. An Executorship-by-the-Numbers, perhaps.

I asked the librarian for assistance. Eager to be helpful, she offered to search titles available in other libraries and to put them on hold. I declined, as I needed the information that day. I went to the bookstore and headed to the business section. I saw many books in passing with eye-catching titles calling my name. Surrounded by books is my happy place, but I had to tell myself to get a grip. There wouldn't be enough hours in the day for any of those over the next few weeks. A quick browse of the business books didn't reveal what I was looking for. I asked the floor staff for help, but all to no avail. I did eventually find a 101 manual but, woe is me, I found it at the very end of my Executor journey. It seemed to pop out of the shelf as I was happily browsing at Chapters, not looking for anything specific: *So You've Been Appointed Executor* by Tom Carter. They say not to judge a book by its cover, but I swear that book was mocking me. Yes, I bought it and read it cover to cover, if only to confirm for myself that I did a great job.

I found the paucity of comprehensive literature on this important topic distressing at the outset, but with persistence, I found enough, mostly browsing the world's fountain of all knowledge— the internet. This helped to glean, if not a clearly delineated road map, at least a general understanding of the process steps. There's a saying: "Give a person a fish and you feed him for a day. Teach a person to use the internet and they won't bother you for weeks, months, maybe years." It worked for me. I found myself totally absorbed in the information available. The research process consumed my days, but it wasn't a penalty. Since my early childhood, my favourite place to be has been between the covers of a book. Learning new concepts from the masters, I had at my fingertips the terminology that would empower me, as well as a great many rules, scenarios, protocols, rituals, financials, taxables, funerals, document samples, and the potential idiosyncrasies of the people involved at every step of the process.

I discovered, to my surprise, that I had the option to resign from the role of Executor. I wasn't obliged to go ahead with it, even though I'd said yes to the appointment and had been named Executor in the will. I think it's important to know this because as our life situation changes, it becomes important to protect our own best interests. We shouldn't feel bad about a change of mind if, having considered the option honestly, the conclusion is that accepting this big commitment at this time is not a good fit.

If I decided to refuse the role, which is formally called renouncing the role, I would have to sign a form called a Notice of Renunciation—a fancy title for a form that says "No." This form would be filed in court, and since there was no alternate Executor named in Marilyn's will, the Court would appoint someone. While I found this information interesting and was still torn about my decision to move forward, I didn't for a minute consider my resignation a viable option. I had been comfortable in my trust with Patrick in the role but didn't want it in the hands of a stranger. There's a world of difference between love and duty, but fulfilling this role fell fully into the realm of both. Having agonized over the decision and now given myself permission to say no if necessary, I believed that my abdication would be a grave betrayal of Marilyn's trust and a blatant disregard for the quality of our fifty-year friendship.

Also, I knew Marilyn's will, having it in hand. It was a thin and simple will. I saw yellow flags of caution but no red flags indicative of anything I'd feel uncomfortable handling. The beneficiaries were young adults I cared about, but I'd still be perceived as a neutral, outside of the family party. Stories abound of family tensions escalating when it comes to dealing with the death of a family member. Perceptions are critical in establishing trust, and I'm convinced, without the benefit of having discussed this with Marilyn, that the potential for conflict in her family and her belief in my ability to manage it was a factor she considered in choosing me to manage her estate. She would have understood that my personality and indoctrination as a medical professional placed me on a life-long path of learning and service to others. She knew, perhaps better than I did, that this set of values applied in this context would lead me to consider first the well-being of the beneficiaries, her beloved grandchildren. She also knew that I would strive for excellence in the role and take pride in the successes that followed.

The literature is of one voice in urging us to be very thoughtful in choosing our Executor and that once appointed, your Executor choice may not be the best choice forever. You may, for example, have chosen someone your own age, but as you get older, so does that person, who may no longer be in a position to take on the role when the time comes. The appointment may need to be changed to ensure a smooth administration of your estate as needs and financial realities change over time. It's also important to make sure to name an alternate should your fist choice no longer be viable.

Short of issuing a warning in bold and colourful lettering stating "Danger. Proceed at Your Own Risk," experts also caution those asked to accept the rich, complex, and multidimensional Executor role to be equally careful in their decision process. It's hard in most cases to say no to a dear friend's request, but executorship is demanding work, and risking your friend's disappointment isn't a good enough reason to accept the role if it's not going to be possible for you to complete the work. In fact, doing so may be a disservice to everyone concerned, so it's critical to consider your response to the invitation carefully.

Retaining a Trust company to act as Executor is put forward in the literature as a strong recommendation. Trust companies market themselves as having people with extensive knowledge about estates and experience in all aspects of estate administration—people with the business knowledge and the capacity to deal with the human issues with understanding and empathy. They also serve as a neutral party should there be a need to facilitate conflict resolution among beneficiaries. A scenario put forward involves choosing a Trust company with a family member as co-Executor. These are interesting options and well worth considering, especially for a large and complicated estate. The cost of this approach is an important factor to analyze in making the decision. The fees a Trust Executor can charge are determined by provincial guidelines and can be significantly less than the fees charged by a lawyer, who may choose to charge his or her regular steep professional hourly rate on all aspects of the estate work, even the menial tasks.

There are likely a number of other factors to think about in weighing the options available in the choice of one's Executor, but when thinking through all this, it seemed to me that Marilyn had made a good choice toward maximizing her legacy.

A clear advantage for me was that I knew a lot about Marilyn's estate. It was straightforward without the complexities of property ownership, businesses, or strange foreign assets—nothing I'd be unfamiliar with. Overnight, I went from a feeling of deep regret and silently cursing my situation to a full commitment, prepared to navigate the demands of this unknown venture and to make the best of it. I wouldn't let my world be limited by fear. After all, a promise is a promise. I was known to keep mine, and as a practice I didn't make one unless I intended to keep it. A promise casually made then broken was despicable, worse than a lie. Following through was not so much a decision as a realization that having given my word, I was now bound to do what I said I would do. I knew from my life experience, including my recent adventure learning to drive in Winnipeg, that the best way to get over doubt and inexperience is to dive in, to jump headfirst into the messy work of learning.

I knew I was neither gifted nor maladroit and also that I wasn't coming at this empty-handed. As a solitary, visual, and kinesthetic learner, I'm good at research and self-study, and with application I get the hang of things. I spent my life this way, collecting initials after my name while working hard to acquire the knowledge and skills I needed throughout my career. In the middle of my anxiety, I was hyper-aware that I lacked the credentials to serve as Executor with authority, but it was dawning on me that I wasn't a complete chowderhead. I had the essential skills needed for this role in ample supply: the courage to engage in the process; the tenacity to learn (I was known to be tenacious and had at times been referred to as a dog-with-a-bone); and the skills to problem-solve along the way, seek advice, and work with qualified professionals as needed so that I wouldn't fly blind. I'd also at times been described as a workaholic with a tendency to push hard and move fast—tendencies I may have to temper, I reflected, on this journey.

My learning curve was steep, but my inquisitive mind was hooked. Something loosened inside me as I read and processed the Executor literature. It was a shift from doubt to wonder about this set of strange but appealing circumstances we don't encounter every day, a clarity of mind that neutralized the uncertainty I'd experienced in the last few days. I was no longer tormented by indecision. I believed I knew enough to master the fundamentals and felt as if I had a new persona; I had become the Executor, committed to the fullness of the role and with one law to live by, a sacred vow, one rule that could not be broken: Thy Will Be Done. I had a mission, a last chance to do something grand for a dear friend who had done so much for me. Of course I could do this! It doesn't take an extraordinary person to serve as Executor. With focus, an ordinary person, yours truly, can complete the process with extraordinary results. Only then, with this flash of insight, did I remember how honoured I'd felt when Marilyn asked me to serve in this role on her behalf.

I knew that the Executor position is not one of prestige. It brings no possibility of selfish benefit except, perhaps, of being able to tell yourself you're doing some big important thing. Be warned: it's demanding work with dozens of factors to consider.

I acknowledged that taking on the role would be a major distraction and wished for better timing. But the stars weren't likely to align any time soon while I procrastinated, stuck in my decision process, I scolded myself. I understood that risk in this context might be a four-letter word not to be ignored, and I acknowledged that the risks, if the Executor made mistakes, could be perilous, but I didn't foresee the likelihood of plunging into jeopardy at any point in my journey. Getting started would be the key to building momentum. I thought of the Irish proverb I love: "You never plough a field by turning it over in your mind. Taking action is where the magic begins."

Emboldened by my readings and reflections, I knew with quiet confidence that I was up for the job, come what may, adverse to failure in this endeavour. My mind was made up as much in reflex as in careful consideration. *This is the right place and the right time. I'll do it*, I decided, now rock solid in my resolve and exhilarated with the powerful desire to do it right…maybe with a touch of foolhardy bravado, not realizing the world of challenges and surprises that awaited me.

3

Friday, November 17, 2017

—

A Journey Into the Unknown

Friday arrived quickly and like any other Friday, except that today was travel day, time to begin the adventure of my appointed journey. *Have appointment will travel*, I thought vaguely and smiled at my own catch-phrase whimsy. I generally dress for comfort these days, wearing athleisure clothing almost exclusively as I hang around the house or walk the neighbourhood park. If it's true that people's personalities and lifestyles can be revealed by the clothes they wear, then move over, Myers-Briggs, I've taken the fashion style test and the results scream one thing only: detachment from the business demands of the world. There's nothing much in my wardrobe that has seen the hot side of an iron since my retirement.

Today I made an extra effort to dress well in honour of the occasion and mostly to look presentable for my first visit with Marilyn. The book cover of *Dress for Success*, the phenomenal best seller of the mid 70s, popped into my mind's eye. Marilyn and I had a well-worn copy. We had chuckled over its premise and debated the pros and cons. Rightly or wrongly, there is a bias to judge and attribute intellectual capability based on how we look. Today I aimed for smart but casual elegance in my travel ensemble: a multicoloured cardigan over a white cotton long-sleeved t-shirt, classic black stretch pants of wrinkle-free fabric styled for all day comfort, and soft leather loafers with a matching shoulder bag and a light-weight but warm wool jacket— perfect for the unpredictable Kelowna autumn weather.

I began my journey prepared for a sojourn of undetermined length in British Columbia, a familiar destination but, given these circumstances, a journey into the unknown. *Travel is always transformative*, I thought, and I hoped for a successful stay. *Starting out will likely be the easy part but staying the course more challenging*, I reflected as I arrived at the airport on schedule after a short taxi ride. I had a few minutes to spare before my flight so, bonus, I made a beeline to Starbucks for a much-anticipated latté.

I appreciate the wonderful world there is to see, and the romance of an adventure, especially with the freedom of air travel, has always appealed to me, even though I'm quite happy in my own back yard and feel no need to search the world for truth or beauty. I have travelled often on vacation and business and do travel still, these days enjoying the sometimes quirky and always fascinating stories of the people I meet along the way perhaps more than the thrill of flight and place.

Yes, I'm that person who greets others in elevators and checkout lines, the one who strikes up a relationship at the airport. It's not a boast to say I can make friends with just about anybody in practically any setting. My family is mystified by this behaviour, which they see as incongruent because they know me as a solitary type who prefers to avoid large social gatherings, a happy introvert who finds magic in solitude and is seemingly immune to loneliness. They call me a people-magnet for what seems to them my extraordinary capacity to attract people's confidence in daily encounters, my ability to connect quickly and deeply with a stranger one-on-one, my superpower. They tease me about the neon sign indelibly stamped in bold letters across my forehead that flashes: "Talk to me."

My sister-in-law, Maggie, had an interesting take on this. She called me an old soul and theorized that those people I connect with are in fact not strangers but people I've known before. Could be. But there's no secret or mystery. I am a social creature. I value meaningful interactions. Very little is more compelling to me than a good story, and I know from experience that everyone has one. The only tool I need to begin what I qualify as a rich and unique adventure in which a perfect stranger becomes a potential friend is a simple smile of genuine acknowledgement. I scan the world around me, absorbing the noise and the colour, which never loses its appeal. But I never have to imagine or invent the life of my fellow travellers. What kind of life does this one live? Where is this one going? Who is this one going to see and why? The people I meet are typically eager to confide intimate details of their lives as if I already know them, or perhaps because they feel safe in the fact that I don't know them at all. Either way, this intimacy fills me with humility and compassion. The exchange is always compelling, and in those brief moments of chance encounter, I am transported, much as I am when reading a great book, beyond my own drama into a world of endless possibilities, a world in which I feel connected to a greater purpose.

Today is no exception. My travel companion, a nurse administrator in cancer care, and I chat happily about our common health care background, current issues in health services delivery, and the brilliant solutions we want to have implemented asap. After a simple question—what brings you to Kelowna today? — she confides:

"I'm going to meet, for the first time, my birth father and adult half siblings. I'm anxious about it but also very excited. At this stage in my life, I need to find them. I feel as though they're calling me."

"How wonderful for you! How did you find each other?"

"My success in finding them is due entirely to the amazing internet resources available to us. Family mystery solved through my life-altering discoveries using Ancestry.ca."

"There he is," she exclaimed as we walked toward the baggage claim. "My father."

"How do you know it's him?" I asked, surprised.

"Easy," she responded with a brilliant smile. "He's quite famous through his distinguished career as captain of the Vancouver Canucks."

Riveted, I watched their joyful first meeting—a major league welcome with smiles, tears, laughter, and the warmest of hugs.

I walked away thrilled that she'd chosen to acknowledge me with her confidences and, in so doing, transformed an encounter with a complete stranger into a surprising and beautiful inter-ruption in what I had anticipated would be a sad journey. Their happy reunion brought a spring to my step as, with my luggage in tow, I went on my way to catch a cab. I hoped I wouldn't come to regret not renting a car as I passed a sign to the rent-a-car-kiosks. Luckily, I caught the first cab in the taxi line. My driver, Raj, shared tales of his journey to Canada and details of his family well beyond the usual pleasantries. I leaned forward in my seat and we chatted non-stop throughout the drive to Marilyn's apartment. Eager to be of service, he opened the lock box at the apartment building and detached it from the gate. I was thankful, and later on a little embarrassed to admit I might have struggled without his help in this relatively simple manual task.

I retrieved the apartment keys and brought the lock box with me. I considered it my job, even though I wasn't yet the Executor, to secure the apartment as the first order of business, a very important step in safeguarding Marilyn's assets. The literature emphasizes the Executor's important duties in protecting the deceased's assets from loss, theft, or destruction and points out that if the estate suffers a loss, the Executor may be held liable for its replacement. A variety of strategies for protecting assets are outlined, including taking items such as cash and jewellery, for example, into your own custody and moving certain assets to secure storage. I didn't think we would need to implement any of these strategies.

Stories abound about the importance of protecting assets, and I was sensitive to this issue. Just recently my friend Betty, who is very conscientious in managing her brother's estate, had a strange experience, even though she'd taken every appropriate measure to protect her brother's assets. Three months after his death, she was shocked to hear from the bank that cheques were arriving with his signature—forged, obviously. He had been severely physically disabled and managed to get around the house slowly with a walker and outside in his farm yard with the use of various pieces of equipment, especially his Kubota. He was an exceptionally friendly man with an open-door policy for the people he knew in his small community. He welcomed anyone who came knocking at his door, not acknowledging his vulnerability. When the person who wrote the cheques in his name was busted, it came to light that on a visit to his home, she had stolen a pack of blank cheques from his kitchen table. Betty, in her role as Executor, could not have prevented this, but I saw the story unfold in my mind as I picked up an extra key on the kitchen counter left there by Marilyn's grandson on a recent visit. I re-counted the keys to make sure I had then all. No one but me would now need a key to the apartment. Had I followed the advice in the books, I would have changed the lock system. That would be overkill, I thought, knowing all the players as I did. I dropped off my luggage, did a quick walk-about the apartment, and decided to head straight to the hospice. I called a taxi and—bonus—Raj, my new friend, was still in the neighbourhood and responded to my call.

We arrived at the Central Okanagan Hospice House on Ethel Street in less than 10 minutes. Hospice House is a free-standing, modern, 24-bedroom, single-storey house surrounded by beautiful gardens. Its location in Kelowna's oldest neighbourhood, within walking distance from downtown and many of the city's best restaurants and shops, makes it easily accessible for patients and their families. It provides end-of-life care for people with advanced disease when cure is no longer possible. I checked in at the reception desk, where a volunteer welcomed me and escorted me to Marilyn's room.

The first person I saw as I entered the room was Michael, Marilyn's youngest son, now 52-years old. "Long time no see," he said, bringing a smile to both our faces as he stood up to greet me with an enthusiastic bear hug. I hadn't seen him in years, because he and his mother had been estranged. He was exactly as I remembered him: tall and squarely built with the swarthy, broad, unlined face of his European heritage. A full head of thick black hair was now streaked with gray, with a thick mustache to match, and dark-brown liquid eyes. He looked comfortably distinguished in his button-down shirt, casual black pants, and black light-weight jacket, fancied up with the punch of top stitching on the pocket edges and looking soft and comfortable enough to sleep in. I always thought he resembled his mother—not so much physically but in the less tangible aspects of personality. The deep dimple in his right cheek reminded me of the beautiful little boy I babysat eons ago, a little boy with a sweetness that was hard to forget. I was thrilled to see him and felt his reciprocity despite our long separation.

"I'm sorry you're having to be the Executor. You've done this before?"

"No, Michael. It's my first time at this job. I'm afraid I'll be improvising and learning at every step. But I'm committed to doing it right."

"Well, improvising can be half the fun. I've never done it either, but I know it's a ton of work and it should have been my job, had I been smarter. I'll help you with anything while you're here. Whatever. Whenever. However. Just say the word," he said as he pulled up a chair for me at the bedside.

His candor was disarming, and I knew instantly with a wave of sweet relief that not only would we get along but that we'd work well together. I couldn't help shooting him a beaming smile.

"Thank you, Michael. I'll appreciate your help, and we'll learn together as we go," I murmured, knowing that while the bond we shared ran deep and true, he would have likely preferred a different scenario had he been involved in the decision process. I was touched by his caring attitude.

I turned my attention to Marilyn. She was covered to her chin, seemingly lost in the single bed she'd come to only three days earlier and which, at first glance, occupied the entire room. I was shocked by her emaciated form, barely recognizing the face I'd befriended for 50 years. Her eyes were closed and shrunken in their sockets. Dry skin pulled too tightly across her cheekbones. Her glossy, fiery red hair, inherited from her Irish mother, was now wispy, all colour drained away and plastered to her scalp. Her breathing was fast and shallow. Always an ample-bodied woman, the pounds had now evaporated, leaving a tiny profile under the covers. She appeared as delicate as a small child. And as vulnerable.

Despite Elena's clear messages, I wasn't prepared for Marilyn's death to be so imminent. I couldn't deny the evidence in front of my eyes and now had a strong sense of how close she was to the end. I was raised to believe there's always hope, but no amount of wishful thinking would change the immutable fact that she wouldn't be going home from here. Was I ready for this? Can one ever be ready to say goodbye to a friend of 50 years? I was grief-stricken, but despite the tears stinging my eyes, I took a deep breath and swallowed in an attempt to compose myself, not wanting a melt-down in the company of strangers. With a lump in my throat and my stomach tied up in knots, I greeted her, injecting in my voice much more spirit than I felt.

"Hello, Marilyn. It's me, Germaine. I'm so glad to be here with you."

I kissed her forehead as tenderly as I would a newborn baby and reached to hold her hand, feeling its coolness beneath the blankets despite the warmth of the room. I was hoping for a response, but there was no evidence that Marilyn heard me or was aware of my presence. Unexpectedly, however, as I held her hand, my anxiety dissipated, and I found my thoughts shifting to peace and acceptance of the inevitable.

As I sat at the bedside absorbing the details of my surroundings, I was struck by the contrast of this space with the one I had recently experienced at Bill's beside at the Health Sciences Centre. The room was bare, basically devoid of colour. It had an aura of peace and tranquility, even though muted voices and soft stepping could be heard from the hallway, and despite the fact that a life here clearly hung in the balance. This was not a place of danger. No emergency button to summon help. No intercom system. No dings, beeps, or rushing of feet to answer codes of various colours. No aggressive death-delaying treatments. No web of IV lines. No electrodes. No feeding tubes. No suction pumps. No ventilators. No monitors with large screens. No warning bells or flashing lights from complicated, impersonal machines. No equipment. Just the bed flanked by a chair on each side and a bedside table. The focus was clearly on comfort care and pain management. I was pleased to see Marilyn's wishes honoured as clearly requested in her Advance Directives.

"She had a better day yesterday," said Michael. "Julia and I were both here. She surprised us by being fully awake for a few minutes. She said we looked great and asked about our health and the kids. She said she loved us and thanked us for being here." He choked up with emotion, clearly worried that those would be her last words.

"I think that's a great memory for her and all of you to treasure, Michael."

What an unfathomable mystery is the human body, I mused, pleased that they were there for this special moment and sad to have missed it.

Melanie, Marilyn's neighbour and long-time friend, was sitting on the other side of the bed, facing me. I appreciated her compassion and companionship at Marilyn's bedside. Still, I think it's fair to admit I felt some awkwardness in visiting with a stranger at the bedside of my friend who was lying there on death's front porch and not in any position to participate. It was all a bit surreal. I didn't want to see her lying there in that state, unmoving, eyes shut. I'm sure Melanie felt the same way. *God*, I prayed, *don't let this happen to me. Please give me a few more years as a healthy, happy geezer and then an instant death like my brother had with his brain aneurysm on the golf course. Zap. Lights out.*

We sat there for a while watching Marilyn, watching each other, not talking, perhaps praying, lost in our own thoughts, immersed in our felt and anticipatory grief and battered by feelings neither one of us wanted. I thought of our Monday night chats, glass in hand, chuckling over the silly events of our day. From there my mind wandered to an image of her last days as a gentle passing, an intimate thing with her loved ones at the bedside, and I wondered what her world will be like, past the pain, on the other side of death. Looking at her, Zachary, who plays Minecraft and Dragon Run would say: "Her energy bar has drained; she is losing all her heart points."

I couldn't take my eyes off her face as I held her hand, hoping that if my gaze didn't waver she would wake up. I wanted to nudge her into wakefulness for one last conversation, however brief. If I pretended long enough, perhaps what was unlikely might end up happening.

In an effort to disguise my dismay as I watched her stillness, I thought about dying as a great mystery—the fears, the courage, the lost love and friendship, the regrets, the longings as we learn to live around pain and sorrow. Then I reflected on how temporary life is and how quickly it's gone. Sitting there, comfortable in my own skin, I was fully aware of my own aging and the increasing limitations that come with age, but I felt no sense of my own mortality. I felt young in so many ways. None of us, I know, have any business taking our lives for granted. Good health is a great gift to be treasured and nurtured every single day. It's everything, really, and it can change overnight.

Time is precious and capricious. But today, in my smug boomer mode, I felt strangely immune to death. I found myself wondering, however, how I would spend the last months, weeks, or days of my life if I knew the end was coming. What words would I say that would be the last thing I ever said? Would the wisdom that comes from experience lead me to slow down to reflect on everything I've accomplished, no matter how small or trivial? Would I feel proud? Or would I feel a kind of immediacy with an awareness of the importance of everything in my day worthy of my full attention? Would I busy myself making every minute count to fill the precious time remaining? The thought of death as so non-negotiable, so inevitable, so permanent made me shudder. I thought of it not as an abstract concept but as a presence that couldn't be denied. It's just a matter of time, really. How should I mark my final transition? All these choices to make. Big decisions. Food for future thought, but in the meantime, I resolved to embrace the cliché: live today as if you're going to die tomorrow. Yes, it's a cliché because it's true.

Melanie and I began a quiet conversation, not a coffee-klatch at the bedside in an effort to normalize the dying process, but the usual exchange when people meet each other for the first time under such circumstances: feeling more than a little tongue-tied and deeply frustrated at seeing their loved one in this state of inevitable death yet wanting to deny its finality and feeling completely powerless to help. We covered the banal details of life. How we knew Marilyn. Where we lived. Where we grew up. Our life's work.

Her sadness palpable, Melanie asked, "Do you think she's aware of our presence?" Does she hear our conversation?"

I was taken aback by her timing and thought it strange, as I was trying to puzzle out the answer to the same question.

"It feels odd to speak as if she weren't present, but there is growing evidence that hearing is the last sense to go in the dying process, and that people who are seemingly unresponsive are aware of what's going on around them and can hear conversations. So I'm thinking Marilyn may well be hearing every word we're saying, even as she's slipping away. One thing I know for sure is that the healthy Marilyn would have been delighted to see her friends get to know each other," I replied. "I believe she does hear us and has enough awareness to feel surrounded by love."

Our conversation was suddenly interrupted by a bout of restlessness and a groan so penetrating that we gasped in unison. I rushed to find a nurse, recognizing this as a sure sign it was time for Marilyn's next dose of pain medications. Everyone left the room as the staff arrived for comfort care.

Until that moment, I hadn't realized it was well past dinner time. My breakfast eaten in haste just before my flight was a long time ago, and my stomach was growling.

"There's a nice sushi house nearby. Let's go for dinner and then I'll drive you home," suggested Melanie.

I accepted Melanie's generous offer, turning to greet Julia, Michael's wife, who had just arrived. She looked great—a very attractive middle-aged woman wearing jeans and a casual autumn jacket with a sense of style. Tall and slim, I imagined she could put anything on and it would suit her. I had no preconceived notion of how she would look after years of no contact, but I remembered admiring her striking looks as a young woman, and that hadn't changed, only matured. Her eyes, the most striking of her elegant features, were of an intense blue with the power to draw you in, warm you up, and make you feel at home. Her friendly demeanour said, "Trust me." I hoped that would be a true reading. We left her and Michael to take a shift at Marilyn's bedside vigil.

We talked about Melanie's brand-new sporty Honda CRV and its amazing features all the way to the restaurant. Funny coincidence, her vehicle was exactly the same, except for its colour, as the one sitting in my garage at home.

The restaurant wasn't busy and we chose a table by a large window. We scanned the menu and ordered quickly, since we were both ravenous. Our conversation continued as we sipped our green tea in the restaurant's relaxed atmosphere. I realized that what had started earlier as a superficial exchange was providing me precious glimpses of Marilyn's life in her community of women friends.

"Marilyn was crazy about Mah-jong," reflected Melanie. "For years, we played with a group of friends every Tuesday afternoon. Sometimes more often. We took turns going to each other's homes. Marilyn has a deluxe game set with ivory tiles in a beautiful hinged and carved wooden case, a gift from her cousin, Ana, who brought it back from a trip to Hong Kong."

"I know that set! It's one of her prized possessions. She brought it with her on a visit to Edmonton a couple years ago. She was so enthusiastic about the game that she insisted on an afternoon of Mah-jong with a group of our local friends. So we gathered at Ana's home and over wine and mini cinnamon buns, Marilyn coached us on the rules of the game. She didn't play. She presided over us and laid down the law. The afternoon disappeared in a flash with much laughter and pauses in the game for stories that simply could not wait to be told."

"Yes," said Melanie. "She was especially happy when she won the dice toss for the east sitting position. She believed it was the prevailing wind that brought her good luck. Of course, we were all superstitious about the game," she said with a chuckle. "We brought trinkets as good luck charms and placed them strategically at the top left-hand corner of our game spot. Marilyn's was a cloisonné, an Irish four-leaf clover. She won many games, but it was more likely because of her skill and strategy than the presence of her four-leaf clover."

En route to Marilyn's apartment after dinner, Melanie said, "I've been there many times. It's really close by."

It was getting dark, however. The sun goes down early in the Okanagan. Silence rode with us in the vehicle, both of us too engrossed on the route to have a conversation. Melanie took the wrong turn, missing the street to the apartment by a couple of blocks. Nonplussed, she tromped on the accelerator, whizzed by a couple of parked cars, veered sharply to the right with tires squealing, onto the sidewalk to reorient herself, turned around in the middle of the road, and drove on, blithely unaware of my hands gripping the edge of the seat in sheer terror, my eyes fixed on the windshield for the anticipated close call. I was braced for disaster.

Holy crap! She is going to have us killed! I bit back a gasp at the horrible image of both of us crushed like large female moths on the windshield. Lucky for us, the traffic gods were on our side, as no other cars chose that time to drive by. Crisis miraculously averted. *Thank the Lord for small favours*, I thought as I exhaled with great relief. We were safe and sound. When I realized I could talk in a normal voice again, I thanked her and wished her goodnight. Then I waved as she drove away, and I watched until her taillights faded, offering my gratitude that we'd arrived in one piece. *No one gets through life without a few bumps in the road*, I thought. I laughed about the hair-raising ride and admired her chutzpah but decided I might not catch a ride with her next time.

It was after eight by the time I got home, but my body knew that coming from Winnipeg, it was really after ten. Unwilling to wait for the elevator, I tackled the stairs two at a time, arriving at the apartment satisfied with my day. As I reached for the doorknob, I heard a friendly hello. An elderly gentleman with an engaging smile was walking toward me.

"I'm Jack," he said as he extended his hand for a handshake. I shook his hand as I sorted out my impressions. He radiated intelligence and seemed full of life, his eyes dancing with the hint of more than a bit of mischief. I liked him immediately.

"Marilyn and I are good friends. Elena told me you were coming, so I've been expecting you. I'm your neighbour from down the hall. Suite 310. Come over for a glass of wine?"

Claiming fatigue, I declined his friendly invitation, gave him a brief update on Marilyn's day, and committed to a visit the following evening.

"I'm here to help," he said. "Let me know what you need. Oh, and I'll bring you the local paper in the morning. I'll knock on the door just to let you know it's here. Don't feel you have to answer."

You might think it strange that the plan was for me to stay in Marilyn's home and sleep in her bed, but it felt perfectly natural to me. Marilyn had insisted that when the time came, I would stay in her apartment and begin the process of organizing her belongings. This request underscored her level of trust in me and, practically speaking, it made sense. I entered the suite, picked up the suitcase I had left by the door, and headed straight to the bedroom. I've observed that bedrooms usually smell of their owner, but there was no evidence of Marilyn there. It was as if she had left not Monday night but some time ago.

I knew from looking around earlier that there was work to do before I could call it a night. The queen-size bed was against the wall under the window, having been pushed there to make space for an electric bed reclaimed by Home Care the day before. The heavy wheel tracks in the carpet and the signed form on the bedside table were the only evidence it had been there. The bed linens were clean and fresh. Elena had seen to that. The room was otherwise sadly neglected, with a variety of pills, including oxycodone, a narcotic of significant street value, scattered on the floor from the bedside table to the closet. My dismay grew as I entered the en suite and saw discarded bandages on the floor, and used catheters and urine bags hanging over the shower faucet in the tub. I felt embarrassment, actually outrage, toward my nursing colleagues whose practice in this case was so disrespectful. The scene was truly cringe-worthy. When did nurses become too posh to wash? I wished I could just close the door to block out the pungent ammonia smell of stale urine. Not possible! The door had been taken off its hinges some days ago to facilitate wheelchair access. I found it leaning against the wall in the den.

I changed into my cleaning duds, opened all the windows—hoping for a breeze to carry away the offensive smell—rolled up my sleeves, pulled on a pair of rubber gloves, and proceeded with a deep cleaning of the bathroom. An hour later, happy with the clean smell of bleach stinging my nostrils, I was ready for bed. One room done. I could check that off my list, happy to note that cleanliness and order prevailed everywhere else in the apartment, from the gleaming kitchen sink to the second bathroom to the living room and den. There was one more thing I simply had to do: find the Mah-jong set and especially the four-leaf clover, which I planned to take to the hospice the next day, a talisman on Marilyn's bedside table. I looked in every obvious place one would keep such treasured possessions, but to no avail. *Oh well*, I thought, *they'll turn up*. I settled in bed, appreciating the feel of cool, smooth sheets against my skin, and the soft comfort of the pillows. I opened a book I was too tired to read so I plugged my phone in its charger and reached over to turn off the lights, ready for my first night's sleep in Marilyn's home. I'd had enough of a day.

4

—

Water under the Bridge

I woke up feeling truly miserable, the sadness over my friend's condition exacerbated by a wicked headache. I needed a cup of strong coffee, which I expected I'd most likely have to catch on my way to the hospice, since Marilyn was a tea drinker. Nevertheless, ever the optimist, I began a search of the cupboards, just in case. The phone rang, and it was Elena, calling to let me know the coffee beans were hiding in the bottom left drawer of the fridge, and the grinder in the lower cupboard by the window. Elena was like that—always a caregiver after years of service as a psychiatric nurse, thinking about everything her people might need. I nearly whimpered, grateful to be among her people.

"You must be psychic, Elena. This is exactly what I need. What a wonderful friend you are. Thanks a million."

I hung up to answer the soft knock on the front door. Jack and his adult son, whom he proudly introduced as Jack junior, or Jackie, were both there to deliver the *Okanagan Weekender*.

47

I made a ceremony of grinding my coffee beans, a medium Columbian blend, pouring the coffee, inhaling deeply as I watched the steam rise with the rich aroma permeating the room, and thinking, *this is what heaven smells like.* In fact, if they don't serve coffee in heaven, I really don't want to go there. I nestled into the overstuffed couch with my gifts of the morning paper and a cup of coffee that I knew could trigger tears of joy. I slurped the first sip with noisy delight and chuckled at this behaviour I could get away with since no one was there to judge. I'm not a coffee snob, but I was certain this was world-class, the best cup to be found in the Okanagan, or perhaps in the known universe. I drank without hurry, enjoying the twin jolts of caffeine and the mild euphoria that was almost immediate. I poured a second cup and raised my mug in a toast to Elena and Jack. I sighed, feeling my headache go away with every sip of this brain-clearing caffeine.

The front page promoted National Child Day and quoted the Conference Board of Canada: "Canada is cheating itself, its kids," it claimed. "For every dollar spent on early childhood support, Canada gets back six dollars in productivity over time."

I cheered loudly, thrilled to see these headlines. I had repeatedly delivered this same message for 20 years in my work promoting children's mental health. On this happy note, I headed to the kitchen in search of breakfast. I trusted there would be no empty fridge syndrome, as Elena had been here. The evidence of her culinary skills and thoughtfulness was evident in the freezer contents. I pulled out beautiful, glossy, mini-Ukrainian cabbage rolls packaged in single-serving bowls and prepared with great anticipation for a morning feast. I greedily stuffed each one in my mouth all in one go. They tasted just like Elena's Baba's, my litmus test for cabbage rolls. Coupled with a serving of classic chili, also found in the freezer—rich and hearty and loaded with vegetables and beans—I enjoyed a perfect meal, albeit strange for breakfast fare. Supported by friends old and new and pampered with a second cup of excellent coffee and a belly full of healthy food, I felt an unexpected sense of well-being. My system had caught up with my schedule, and I was ready for whatever the day would bring.

Kelowna is a city in the southern interior of British Columbia that serves as the gateway to the stunning Okanagan Valley. With its mild winters, it's famous as a retirement community, which is what drew Marilyn and Richard there upon his retirement. It's also famous for its lush orchards and many wineries, which deserve more than one visit. With its location on Okanagan Lake, it's one of Canada's top summer destinations—a hotbed for outdoor activities and a virtual playground. Bill and I loved the Okanagan. We shed the weight of our Alberta winter and drove there for a great vacation, which included precious time with Richard and Marilyn and the boys, every summer during our children's growing up years. I didn't plan on sightseeing this visit, however. I called a taxi to the hospice.

Marilyn was much the same as the day before, just barely alive. I wondered what her last meal was. I wanted to ask Elena, but I wouldn't, worried she would find the question upsetting. I was comforted knowing Marilyn wouldn't be feeling hungry.

After greeting Marilyn, I sat across the bed facing that day's visiting friend, Gloria.

"I know you," she said with a beautiful smile. "Marilyn often spoke about your shared nursing history." After a brief pause, she said candidly, "Marilyn and I were in a counselling group together several years ago. We were both looking for ways to cope with the loss of our husbands. We made a real connection that was therapeutic for both of us and have been friends ever since."

Lily breezed in after lunch. She and Marilyn had worked as colleagues in a local continuing care centre through which they had developed a 20-year friendship. Her bubbly laughter and sparkling eyes brought her stories to life.

"We holidayed together in Palm Springs last winter," she said. "That was a big highlight in our journey together."

The hours passed quickly, and I felt deeply moved by these shared confidences, each story a privilege to hear. I left mid-afternoon, having planned the next day with Michael. Our aim was to have someone keeping vigil with Marilyn if not all the time, at least most of the time. Michael, Julia, and their adult children, Mia and Trevor, as well as Lily, planned on being there most of the following day. I don't know if she heard me, but I promised Marilyn I'd be back the next evening to tuck her in and read her a bedtime story. I kissed her forehead and both cheeks, and as I turned to leave, I was startled to see what had escaped my attention until that point—the only personal item in the room, Marilyn and Richard's wedding picture on the bedside table, with Bill and me standing beside them as Best Man and Maid of Honour. Tender memories.

Michael drove me home. As we entered the vehicle, he surprised me with this question in an anguished tone, his dark eyes smoldering: "Why didn't you tell me?"

"I don't know what you mean, Michael. Why didn't I tell you what?" I asked, taken aback.

"Why didn't you call to tell me she was so sick? I should have been told long ago," he said, his voice vibrating with distress and rising as if there was a problem with my hearing. His shoulders edged forward toward the steering wheel, carrying seven years of sorrow. He was clearly fuming and fighting a mighty battle for a grip on his emotions. After years of study and practise, I consider myself an excellent observer of behavioural cues that betray emotional states and was prepared to witness grief demonstrated in a wide range of behaviours. I now saw grief, regret, and sorrow mixed in with the anger he directed at me. I relaxed my arms, which I realized I had folded squarely across my chest as a subconscious self-protective gesture. Defensiveness would not help defuse this situation.

"My kids are devastated that they weren't informed until the end."

I felt compassion for his position and searched for my voice, for a mot juste beyond my own small words, for a delicate way to reach him, to bring him comfort. I couldn't tiptoe around his feelings, and there was no benefit in being evasive. Acutely aware of the sensitivities, I settled for simple words and simple truths.

"I'm sorry, Michael. Marilyn had given strict instructions not to call you and your brother. I know she was very close to your kids, and I'm sure she would have had something important to say to all of you. She would have found words of love and pride and dreams for your futures without her. I know this because she shared these thoughts with me, and I know she saw her job as a grandparent to shield her grandchildren from the painful realities of her declining health. I wish things could have been different, and I'm glad Elena called you when she did, but she couldn't do it either until she got Marilyn's permission."

Marilyn had told me about the big blow-up in the Safeway parking lot, where Michael had accused her of spending her money foolishly. She talked about how she had become guarded, then angry, then aggressive in her rejection. Harsh words. Powerful words were spoken, and unshakeable boundaries were set. This incident had served as the catalyst for the heartbreaking severance of bonds previously held sacred, the estrangement of seven years and holding. I'm sure there was much more to the story, but she wouldn't talk about the details, claiming it too painful to think about.

My understanding of the situation has deepened over time as I've seen similar struggles in a number of families in my own circle of people I know. Still, I've never believed severing contact to be a productive way to handle a family conflict because of the inevitable devastating impact on everyone involved. I know from experience that when feelings are put on the table, talked out, and examined from a different perspective, they often lose their impact. Marilyn and I had tentative conversations about estrangement being a loss no matter how one looks at it, but those attempts really led nowhere. And here I was somewhere in the middle of it but in no way prepared to pass judgement. I forced back a swell of sadness. Today, no matter how much I wished they had reconciled both for her benefit over time and for Michael's, so much had stood between them. Ugly words spoken in haste. Hard feelings not put to rest, leaving a gap between them neither could find the give and take to close.

"Michael, Marilyn's words were, 'It's all water under the bridge.' That's what she said to Elena." She had finally pressed the reset button, making space for reconciliation, for peace, before her final exit. "'Please do call Michael,' she'd said."

He seemed to move quickly past his paralyzing emotions and to connect to his own wisdom as he said:

"I know I'm feeling fragile right now, and each moment with her is precious. I don't blame you. I'm just mad at myself for being such an ass. I could have done something to change this situation long ago. Then I wouldn't be filled with regret for things I've left undone."

"I get it, Michael, and I'm glad you told me how you feel. I hear your sadness and regret. It hurts to lose family without a chance to say a proper goodbye. I'm sorry things have unfolded this way."

This wasn't about me, but I heard in Michael's words an echo of my own feelings. *You're not alone*, I thought, but I didn't say out loud. I've been there. I wish I'd done things differently too. I wish I'd come sooner while Marilyn was still able to have a conversation. I felt like I hadn't been there for her when she needed me most.

I didn't want to leave this encounter with Michael without helping him find a way to make peace with his mother, to feel better in some way. His evident love for her, unbroken by the silence of seven years, further endeared him to me. I understood our conversation to be a sentinel event alerting me to his considerable level of distress. I searched for something wise to say, a healing nugget to console, to move his mountain of grief, but the words failed me, and the moment was lost as we arrived at the apartment and Michael began to unload the boxes he'd brought for the packing to begin. What happens when words fail us? Turns out it's not the end of the world. Sometimes just being a sounding board can be the most helpful thing. I don't think Michael expected anything brilliant. He just needed to share his private sorrows and be heard. Perhaps enough had been said, I mused, hoping this exchange had strengthened our bond.

The phone was ringing as I entered the apartment. It was the pharmacy ready to deliver Marilyn's next batch of blister packs. I had to tell them she would no longer need their services.

A quick lunch then this dogsbody got to work sorting and cleaning the medicine cabinets and collecting pills carelessly dropped on the bedroom floor. Marilyn, who always kept a meticulous home, would be horrified to see this disarray in medications, including the powerful OxyContin that should be treated with utmost respect; all of it was once life-saving, but now it was garbage ready for the pharmacy disposal system.

I turned on classical music full blast, intent on relieving the oppressive silence, and moved on to the closets for an inventory and sorting of Marilyn's personal effects. I had a hard time with this task, having always had a zealous respect for individual privacy, even more so when it involved someone I cared about. Going through the pockets of her garments felt like an enormous invasion of her privacy, a feeling perhaps so intense because, down the street, Marilyn was still alive. But, I reasoned, it had to be done. Marilyn was fastidious about her appearance and stylish although conservative in her choices. *What will I do with all this?* I needed to decide what was bound for charity. *Who could use this line-up of beautiful clothes, several pieces with the price tag still attached, and brand-new shoes nestled in their boxes?*

Satisfied with the tasks accomplished, I settled into the deep comfort of the couch with my dinner and a cup of peppermint tea, enjoying the lovely apartment flooded with sunlight through the open horizontal blinds of otherwise unadorned windows.

After dinner, as promised, I knocked on Jack's door, ready for a moment of relaxation with a new friend, an hour away from all the things I didn't want to think about. His unit was a mirror image of Marilyn's but on the opposite side of the building overlooking the parking lot. It was pristine in its order and cleanliness. I was fascinated by the striking collection of translucent, blanc-de-chine porcelain figurines not so much prominently displayed as strategically placed in his living room, a soft blessing emanating from them. I wanted to touch them but didn't dare. He proudly described them as Quan Yin, collected over several years, each as a memento of a shared celebration with his recently deceased wife.

"Quan Yin is the Oriental goddess of mercy and compassion," he said as I gushed with delighted praise on her beauty. "I enjoy looking at her and feel safe in her company."

"She has been called many different names, depending on one's religion and culture, Jack, but your Quan Yin is my Mother Mary, the personification of unconditional love—the one who hears the cries of the people. She is a great protector. No wonder you feel safe in her presence."

Looking at his collection, I was overcome with a sense of kinship with Jack and a depth of peacefulness that defies explanation. I accepted the wine he offered me, and over a glass of local chardonnay, we began an easy conversation.

"So who are you, Jack? I'd love to know your background." And that was all the prompt it took to dive into his youth.

"At fourteen, I was living on my own," he said, his lips twitching as if he knew something he wasn't going to tell me. I let him take his time. I didn't mind waiting. I was in no hurry. And then he obviously decided to trust me.

"I had to be smart to fend for myself, living on little more than my wits. Hopping trains for fun with my buddies. Catching odd jobs in downtown Vancouver working for a copper penny. Doing anything for a meal. Anything that would pay a little and where the boss didn't ride our ass. Collecting farts in the Chinese laundry to make ends meet."

"What did you do next?" I asked, chuckling like any seven-year-old at his fart reference and enjoying his chattiness. He had my full attention.

He took a sip of wine and said, "I decided that joining the army would be a great gig. But after a three-year stint, I'd had enough of that crap. I came home and lucked into a job in Prince George. There I learned to rebuild motors in Caterpillars and trucks. I would strip the motor, rebuild it, paint it, and send it on."

"That sounds like complicated work. How did you learn the trade?"

"No school learning for me! I learned every darn thing I know by watching. I watched my boss in the shop. I did what he did. Experience is the best teacher, you know. Soon enough, I could do all of it on my own with no one around. Didn't need supervision. No siree, Bob!"

"And you got married while you worked in Prince George?"

"Yes. I was 22-years old when I got married. We were married 58 years. I miss her, you know."

"After all that time, Jack, you must miss her for sure. Where did you live?"

"My wife and I decided to build a house. We didn't have a pot to piss in or a window to throw it out of, but we did it, 20 and 30 dollars at a time. The house is still standing strong today, I'm proud to say. We did a damn good job."

I loved not only his humour but his warmth and forthright simplicity, his boundless amiability. I thought each one of his stories earned him the right to tell another and appreciated that in about 20 seconds, we went from being strangers down the hall in an apartment building to being friends who shared something important.

"But I'm doing all the talking," he observed. "You live in Winnipeg. Marilyn lives here. How do you two know each other?"

"Marilyn was my first Head Nurse when I graduated from nursing school 50 years ago. We worked on a brand new 28-bed unit. Actually, we opened a new hospital building that had four such units in it. Our unit was called 10-2. The building was purpose-designed for patients with serious mental illness—people with depression or schizophrenia, for example. I had a lot to learn as a brand-new grad, and Marilyn was an amazing boss and mentor. We struck up a friendship that has lasted across provinces all these years. It takes effort to hold friends close, Jack, but the distances didn't break us."

"You of all people would understand my son's situation," Jack said, now very serious. "He's a brittle diabetic and severely developmentally delayed. He's 55-years old and has lived with me and my wife all his life. We've had a few tough breaks, that's for sure. You wanna hear a crazy story? After a few years in Prince George, my company transferred me to Kamloops, where we decided to buy a condo. Shortly after we moved in, the property manager came over to tell us we'd have to sell and move out. Can you believe that bugger had the nerve to show up in my house?" he exclaimed with remembered outrage.

"But why would he do that?" I asked.

"The management company had noticed that Jackie was 'retarded.' That's what they called it. They were afraid of him. He was only 12-years old, for God's sake. A little boy. So gentle you'd have been challenged to find a fighting bone in his body. It was clear that they worried about appearances. Having a 'retarded' boy on the premises would take away from the appeal of the condo property. You see what I'm saying? The bastards gave us their demands in writing. Goddam it," he said.

"They could stick their demands where the sun don't shine. We got ourselves legal advice. We appealed through Human Rights and won our case. But the win wasn't worth diddly-do. In the end we did sell and moved on. No one in the complex would talk to us. We were completely ostracized. We had no quality of life in that condo complex."

I didn't have to reach in too far to know how that story made me feel. I felt a well of sympathy, nearly weeping at such human cruelty. This appalling behaviour wasn't an isolated incident nor a work of fiction but it happened right here in Canada, where the stigma attached to those with visible disabilities and mental illness is still alive and well. We talk a good game about inclusion but still don't put our money where our mouth is. I was reminded of how often I'd struggled with similar situations in my psychiatric nursing career.

At this point, Jackie, who'd been in his room watching a movie, came out to say goodnight. He had the same build as his father, but while Jack was strong, wiry, and tough, Jackie looked thin, frail, and delicate. They did, however, have the same brilliant smile. He greeted me in a matter-of-fact manner, as if he'd known me all his life, and announced, "Dad, it's time for my insulin."

Dad excused himself to tend to his son's bedtime treatment. Ever practical, he then showed me where to find the mailboxes and the access for the recycling and garbage systems inside and outside the building. He also gave me the contact information for the property manager.

As we did a walk-about, he showed me Marilyn's parking spot right beside his.

"I knew when she went out because I could hear her in the hallway. I watched at my window for her return to help bring in her groceries. She's needed a lot more help in the last few months. We had many laughs together," he said with a cackle. "I liked that she never shied away from saying, 'Are you fucking kidding me!'"

I reacted with surprise at these words, because in my 50-year relationship with Marilyn, I had never heard her salty vocabulary. Don't get me wrong—I'm a good person, not a prude, and I don't judge people who curse. Like Jack, I accept that there's a time and place when swearing is inevitable, and I even enjoy a little irreverence without outrage or offense.

That night, tucked in the comfort of Marilyn's bed, I reflected on my good fortune in having had her in my life for so many years. I missed her telephone voice. Her telephone laugh. I missed our conversations that had become somewhat predictable but never boring. The familiarity was comforting. And this week I was getting to know her through all the different lenses of her local friends, including Jack, who welcomed me with such generosity. I found it fascinating to think of her life having an impact on all these other lives and wondered what marks would be left on them. I also realized there was no dancing around the truth; I had missed big chunks of Marilyn's life. Our visits and phone conversations, despite a reservoir of good intentions, had far from yielded the entire story, nor would they have even if they had been more frequent. Gritty grief surfaced, and I found myself desperately wanting one more chat.

5

Sunday, November 19, 2017

—

The Pain of Loss

Morning came early. I heard the soft knock on the front door even before I opened my eyes. The morning paper had been delivered. I chose to ignore it and turned to look at the clock. It was almost seven. Mornings were never my time of day. I smacked the snooze button for ten more minutes of lazy-bones bliss while really wanting a couple more hours in bed. That was not in the cards. I wanted to get a lot done that day so that I'd have the whole evening with Marilyn. I planned to pick up a magazine on the way to the hospice and read for her what she never tired off—the latest, juiciest gossip about the Royals.

If the secret to getting ahead is getting started, I figured I'd better get going. No grass would grow under my feet that day. I would start packing, but first things first. I made my bed with carefully mitered hospital corners, a daily discipline I developed in my first month of nursing school and have maintained since. It would have been easy to forego this practice given the numerous tasks on my plate, but in my view a well-made bed, not the state of your kitchen's bottom drawers, as some people think, is a sign of an organized mind, of a manageable day ahead. Once I made the bed, the place was mine. Alone, away from home, grieving and immersed in the unknown, I needed that sense of order to my day.

I then read the morning paper over a quick breakfast and my morning jolt of caffeine, now completely awake and ready to tackle whatever needed doing. The front page, "Homes in Kelowna not Getting any Cheaper," emphasized the need to create affordable housing for seniors, single families, and the 233 homeless people in Kelowna. The article prompted a mind-jump to Marilyn's beautiful high-end condo in downtown Kelowna. She sold it three years ago, taking advantage of what she described as a seller's market. I came to help her pack for the move to her current rented apartment. Marilyn was ruthless in discarding everything she insisted she didn't like or she'd never need again. Marie Kondo would have been proud! She sold items on Kijiji. She donated to charity. She had a massive garage sale. She bartered items with her neighbours. She was precise in her packaging of various gifts for her grandchildren and, sharpie always at hand, she labelled each box meticulously with their name in bold black ink. Then she made notes on a pad directing future dispositions. I remember watching this behaviour with increasing concern, and as the personalized boxes piled up, I became convinced she was death-cleaning. The icing on the cake was when she handed me two of her most beautiful tablecloths to take home with me.

"I don't entertain anymore," she'd said. "I won't need these."

I felt compelled to initiate a suicide assessment, which had Marilyn in stitches and assuring me I could safely leave my nursing cap at the door. I now wondered if she had secrets then about her health that she wasn't prepared to share.

Preoccupied with these thoughts, I resumed my work in the bedroom closet with the intent of filling boxes with select items for future distribution. I retrieved a carton of Marilyn's favourite soap stashed in the back of the closet—six bars of her signature brand wrapped in black paper and hand crafted with a fragrant blend of organic green tea, coconut oil, and activated charcoal. The scent immediately triggered a memory of Marilyn's laughing face as I teased her about her black beauty bars.

"You can laugh all you want," she'd asserted with a chuckle. "Those bars are the secret behind my cheeks' rosy glow."

That discovery especially brought Marilyn's presence into the room; her scent, her colours, the things she treasured, and the packing became not a task but a moving meditation on the woman who was my friend.

The piece de resistance, however, was a large item wrapped in a black felt blanket leaning against the wall at the very back of the closet and held securely straight by the rows of clothing in front of it. My curiosity was piqued. I pulled out the mystery package and leaned it against the bed as I carefully removed the wrapping. Out popped a wonderful piece of art. Untitled. Not numbered. Acrylic on canvas. A painting of an Ojibway Shaman in vivid, intense shades of browns, reds, blues, pinks, greens, and ochre, the shapes delineated in thick black outlines. Stunned, I stepped back, staring at this painting that was so unexpected a find in Marilyn's home. I recognized it as a Norval Morrisseau masterpiece. The famous artist had been the subject of intense media attention. His style was completely unlike any of the art in Marilyn's' collection. *Where did she get this painting, and why is it hidden in the closet?* I wished Marilyn could tell me that story. Perhaps Michael would know.

Lunch time was announced with a knock on the front door. I closed the bedroom door to keep this amazing find a joyful surprise. Julia, ever beautiful with her long black hair and piercing blue eyes, had arrived with hamburgers and fries for everyone. Her 20-year old twins, Mia and Trevor, were with her. The two of them, together with their 21-year-old cousin, Jason, who lived in Grande

Prairie, Alberta, were to inherit Marilyn's estate. I knew all three of them as interesting and delightful young people, having watched them grow up over the years through my visits with Marilyn. I had invited Mia and Trevor to come over to help with the apartment contents—to select the items that were meaningful to them and that they wanted to keep, and to share their thoughts on disposal of the rest. I had already talked on the phone with Jason, who wanted nothing more than one of the matching living room chairs upholstered in a soft rose silk moiré fabric. His girlfriend, Nicole, had fallen in love with those on a visit last summer.

A tour of each room triggered many decisions.

"I have a great surprise for you," I said as we approached the bedroom.

"Tada, take a look at this." I opened the room with a flourish.

Mia stopped in her tracks, exclaiming in a puzzled tone full of disdain as the others remained silent: "What is it? It looks rather primitive."

"It's a Norval Morrisseau," I said, my voice full of reverence. "You must google him. He's an immensely talented and famous Canadian artist honoured with the Order of Canada for his outstanding achievements. This painting could be worth a lot of money," I said, fingers crossed behind my back. "We'll have to do some research to find out if it's an original. I'll follow-up on that for sure."

While I was still in awe, it was clear that I was the only one impressed with the painting and excited about its potential value. They hadn't been exposed to this artist's work and were frankly baffled by my enthusiasm.

We packed a dozen more boxes, making plans for their eventual distribution and chatting amicably. All agreed that the clothing, cosmetics, and various personal items could be donated to Melanie's church group.

"I checked with Melanie," said Julia. "Her church gratefully accepts such items and then sells them to support various charities."

By mid-afternoon, I was yearning to trade in the work of packing for a breath of fresh air, but first I needed to call Ana about the painting. I chose Ana because she was in the art world with her husband, who was a very talented artist. Also, as Marilyn's cousin and close friend, she would want to help. We connected at the first ring and she readily agreed to make inquiries, but she needed details, which I emailed her:

> The painting is 35 by 43 inches. It's beautiful as you'll see in the attached photo. It's in great condition wrapped in a black cloth and hidden, untouched, at the back of the closet for years. Thanks a million for agreeing to work on this. As you can imagine, my days are full and I appreciate all the help I can get.
>
> BTW, there was a newspaper article some years ago stating that only the Morrisseau Family Foundation has the right to authenticate his work. So I'm thinking we'll need to authenticate the authenticators :) The Art Dealers Association of Canada may be able to give us advice. Maybe?

She was already on task, emailing me back with an article dated February 28, 2010 from the *First Nations Drum* newspaper. The article sang his praises as one of the genius painters of his generation.

"He has died leaving a legacy no other artist has left since Pablo Picasso."

Unfortunately, it went on to say:

"His work is now being defamed by painters of low character attempting to cash in on his reputation by selling forgeries done in Morrisseau's style and selling them as originals. The Norval

Morrisseau Heritage Society, an association responsible for putting the stamp of authenticity on Norval's work, has issued warnings about forgeries popping up everywhere. The Art Dealers Association of Canada has stopped issuing certificates of authenticity for any paintings credited to Norval Morrisseau."

We were both intrigued and, undeterred, Ana was committed to following up with her network.

I ventured out for a brisk, refreshing walk, enjoying the sites and landscapes of the prosperous town despite the late November chill penetrating my autumn coat. I stuck my fingers, quickly turning into icicles, deep in my pockets and hugged myself to keep warm as I headed back, planning to be on my way to the hospice right after a quick snack. The phone was ringing as I entered the apartment, the sound echoing, it seemed with urgency, in the quiet space. I rushed to the kitchen to pick up the line. A nurse at the hospice was calling to say that Marilyn had just passed away, peacefully as she slept, at 1730 hrs. She expressed her condolences and asked if I wanted to come over.

"Don't feel you have to," she said. "It's entirely optional. Springfield Funeral Home will be here to pick up her body within the hour. Also, they'll call you in the morning to set up a meeting with you."

Hearing the news was harder than the dread of hearing it. Why had Marilyn chosen this moment to leave us, one of the few times when no one was with her? I was devastated. I felt I had lost the very skeleton that had, to date, held me together. Sinking into the kitchen chair, all I could say was, "Thank you, I'll call you back."

I was torn. Should I go? I had no qualms about sitting with the dead, but I struggled with what my role should be. I believed that Marilyn was no longer there, that her essence was already somewhere else, somewhere I couldn't reach, and that only her shell remained. I didn't feel a capacity to say goodbye at this point.

Will I be less of a friend if I don't go?

Will I be forever wracked with guilt?

Will it be an intolerable breach of my life-long traditions?

This was my first experience of responsibility for burying the dead but not my first experience of loss. At my age, as a member of the "silver tsunami," I want to say, "Of course!" No one can live this long and not have run the gamut of heartbreaking loss, pain, grief. We all know what it is to hurt. The truth, naked and cold, is that we bleed. We cry. We're all on a collision course with death, and the obituary pages are all too often graced with the names and stories of my family, friends, colleagues, and acquaintances, some taken suddenly, others slowly and painfully. All of them are with me now, each added to the endless procession of loss upon loss. Another weight to carry for a cumulative effect that never goes away, an ever-present shadow eating at me from the inside out, a part of me disappearing with every death. I've felt at times that the universe is ganging up on me, yet I've learned to cope somehow, helped by the awareness that nothing but living lightens the burden of loss, and that each of these people I've loved lives on with me. It's not possible to lock their presence away. I know they would want to be remembered with joy and to think that I'd find comfort in calling on them from time to time.

This last question, however, took me back to my first recollection of sitting up with the dead at the time of my grandmother's death, when most of the funeral preparations happened at home. It was a foggy memory, the gaps fleshed out with stories told by my siblings. I was nine-years old, and it was a childhood experience indelibly etched in my memory. My mother had prepared her mother's body, which, once placed in the hand-made coffin, was displayed for viewing in the living room of her home. As a three-day vigil began, this room, in my child's eye, became the death room. Family members, friends, and neighbours gathered to celebrate her life and to pay their respects. There was much noise in the kitchen where the socializing took place—sounds of stories, weeping, condolences, sympathies, comforts. But all was quiet by the coffin, where no conversation was expected. There it was fine for us, in turn, to sit, pray, and soak in the stillness. At intervals during the day and evening, everyone would gather to pray the rosary, their humble and deeply felt request to God to lead my grandmother's soul to the glories of heaven.

The wake was followed by a Catholic celebration the entire community attended. In keeping with the traditions of the time, my grandmother's open casket was positioned just below the pulpit in full view of the mourners. I judge that practice harshly, in retrospect, as adding another point of emphasis on the loss for the bereaved. High mass was celebrated in the ancient language of the church, the mysterious chants music to my devoted child's ears. I was entranced and, as the fragrant aroma of the incense rose followed by the bread of communion, I felt a sense of mystery, of awe, of virtue, purity, and love; I felt in touch with the holy.

I loved everything about my church as a child—the smell of the flickering candles, the statues of Mary and Joseph, the soft light streaming through the stained glass windows lighting up the stations of the cross, my parents and siblings beside me, extended family and friends filling several of the pews polished and scarred with use, the rituals of the special celebrations, the prayers, the hymns, the responses of the congregation spoken in unison. All of it filled me with love and wonder. My mind wandered now, full of guilt, over my fall as an adult away from the religious practices of my growing-up years. I don't reject these entirely because I think of them as integral to who I am. I miss the intensity of my childhood faith. I even grieve the loss of the mystery of it and at times yearn for the ritual, the order, the traditional rites, and the community. I go to church for special celebrations, mostly in deference to the memory of my mother and father, God rest their souls, who were deeply religious and who, more importantly, were the epitome of all that is good in people.

I have experienced this state of bliss that marked my childhood since then, but only once. The experience of it is crystal clear. My husband and I are on a summer vacation, travelling through the Maritimes with our two children, six and seven years old. We've just left the spectacular Cabot Trail, having spent the afternoon at the Alexander Bell National Museum, and lucked in to an overnight stay at the Inverary Inn in Baddeck, a lovely resort stretching along the shores of the Bras d'Ors lake, a place of great natural beauty. We are heading to the park, soaking in these stunning surroundings, when we stumble upon a tiny A-line chapel on the resort grounds. It feels to me so compelling I decide to stay awhile, letting my family take off at a run to play. Sitting there alone, impervious to my surroundings, I am suddenly and inexplicably transported to a place filled with grace and immense peace. It's an unexpected blessing upon my soul. The transcendent experience passes too quickly, interrupted by my children's voices calling. I realize it is way past their bedtime. As I tuck them in, I feel deeply happy. I feel a profound experience of perfect love for these two beings, the intensity of which stays with me throughout and beyond what I've always thought of as, hands down, the best vacation of my life.

I'd never shared this story, mostly because I'd forgotten about it until that moment as it ran through my head like a video. How I wished I could recapture that feeling at that stressful moment when I needed comforting and guidance.

Church celebrations in my youth didn't accept the offering of a eulogy, but the priest's thoughtful homily spoke of everlasting life, of eternal rewards, words that weren't standard lines but messages of inspiration. His appreciative references to my grandmother's qualities and contributions were spoken, as my older siblings speak of it, to comfort, to soothe, perhaps to inspire us, the living, the aggrieved. The pallbearers then carried the coffin out of the church for the procession to the graveyard, followed by a gathering for social support over lunch.

The voice in my head was hammering past my reminiscences; these stories and memories I'd never talked about were now sneaking out of my eyes and rolling down my cheeks.

Will my non-attendance be seen as disregard for the sacredness of Marilyn's body?

Will I be negligent in my duties as Executor if I don't go?

I heard no eloquent answers to my silent questions, but there was also no judgement, only the need for a decision that just wasn't forthcoming. To say I felt at a loss is no exaggeration. I was paralyzed by accumulated grief and utterly consumed with uncertainty, spinning in a panic of indecision and now on the floor, on my knees, and with my Catholic background mysteriously reasserting itself, praying the rosary, past the Apostle's Creed, past the Our Father, to the Hail Mary in the only language I know those prayers: the comforting French language of my childhood, my language of family, friendship, love, music, beauty. Mine was a simple entreaty, through gasping sobs, not for Marilyn's soul but for myself, for help in making the right choice.

It's tough as hell to hold on to your dignity, take my word for it, when you're a weeping mess in a fetal position on the kitchen floor, blinded by your glasses dripping with bitter tears. I know that it's appropriate to cry when someone you love has died, yet I ask as I write: What happened to my tough skin? Looking at this sorry spectacle of myself, I felt shame at how poorly I seemed to cope. In retrospect, as my memory comes back into focus on that night, I imagine Zachary looking at me with his thick-lashed, water-clear hazel eyes as he tells me I need lessons in dignity, and I fight the urge to squirm. He told me one day that his little brother, Noah, needed lessons in dignity because he spent his weekend as a crybaby.

"He was crying for nothing," he said with great disdain.

Why my grief chose this moment to flatten me remains somewhat of a mystery. Why was I such a basket case? Was it the pain from my accumulated losses choosing that moment to explode into a full-blown breakdown? It was not like me—not the imperturbable facade I've been known to maintain even through the moments in my life when I've felt weak. I coasted through stress in my leadership roles, thriving on tight scheduling, the quick pace with ever impending deadlines, the confusion of a busy organization, multiple details competing for attention, crises to resolve that served to keep me alert, sharp, interested. Perhaps a bit smug about seeking the challenges I always accepted, courted even, thinking life would be rather dull without them, I could eat pressure for breakfast and cocoon with it at night as I aimed for perfect outcomes with great confidence. I understood this not as a soft skill but as the essential spark that underscored my long list of successes.

Who is that imperfect person on the floor? There are times when seeing is not enough to make sense of things. This is such a time. I reach deep inside myself to find that I can look at her now, as I write, with compassion: a woman feeling alone in the world and once again battered by grief.

"I need an answer," I begged. "Please tell me what to do."

With this question, just as the panic had started abruptly, it stopped. My brain did an odd thing. It fired off this succinct and profoundly helpful message with the effect of a forehead smack: "Hey, word to the wise—your traditions are not the same as Marilyn's."

What then would be the best way to respect her wishes?

As I called on her to tell me what she wanted me to do, I remembered our conversations and the instructions in her will for her after-death care to be handled by the health care team and the funeral home. The decision-crisis was over.

After this brief but tortured debate with myself, I called the hospice and, finally feeling on solid ground, took a deep and shaky breath and told them I believed Marilyn was in good hands. I would not be coming in. I thanked them for their excellent care, finding comfort in entrusting Marilyn's body to their professional expertise.

My heart shivering with loss, I thought, *She will no longer have the aggravation of the pain and the waiting.* Marilyn had often talked about how draining the rollercoaster ride of her disease and its treatments were as cancer ran rampant throughout her body for nearly a decade. While she worked hard to keep her courage and spirits up, she had reached the end of her endurance, finding the long waits unbearable and everything in her day just another form of waiting. To see the specialist. For test results. For a diagnosis. For a treatment plan. For a surgery date. For the home care nurse who couldn't show up until the next day with the support she needed now, not tomorrow. For relief from the pain-wracked prison her body had become. For the welcome release of death. She would no longer have to wait. Her journey with us was complete.

I called Michael. He already knew, having also received a call from the hospice.

"I'm especially glad that Julia and Mia and Trevor were with me for a visit today. We all had a chance to say goodbye. She chose to die at dinner time," he observed. "As you know, that was always her favourite time of day."

For an instant I was intensely angry with Marilyn for this choice of timing. She knew I was coming. Why couldn't she wait until after my visit? I knew immediately how irrational that thinking was. Equally irrational was my guilt over not having been there with her for those last intense moments. We've all done this, I know—held impossible expectations. For a second I wondered if I'd soon start talking to myself, or perhaps transition from a social to a solo drinker, indulging in fine Okanagan wine for breakfast.

From there my mind switched to gratitude. I was glad I was there at her bedside toward the end, even if I wasn't there as death won the day and she drew her last breath. Being at her bedside had been a unique and extraordinary opportunity.

I shook my head and said, "I agree, Michael. It's great that you had this day with her. She loved you all very much. And yes, she chose to go at dinner time and on a Sunday. She loved nothing more than having us all around her table, especially on Sunday nights. We did have wonderful meals together. She was such an accomplished cook and hostess." After a pause I continued. "She had the dignified death she longed for, don't you think, Michael? No heroics."

Condolences and offerings of support count for a lot at a time of loss, but neither Michael nor I felt the need for trite words of condolences, especially over the phone. We made a plan. Michael would call his brother who lived in Edmonton, Jason, their cousins, and Marilyn's local friends as well as the extended family she'd kept in touch with in Germany. That covered everyone other than the business contacts I'd seen listed in the address book on her desk. I would call Elena, Patrick, Ana, and Jack. And of course I would call home.

"Have a good night," he said. "I'll pick you up tomorrow to go to the funeral home."

My calls completed, with condolences conveyed as best I could, the reality hit me hard. I knew I couldn't dodge the accumulated pain. Dinner was now out of the question. Unable to comfort myself even with a cup of tea, I went to bed.

.

6

—

First Day on the Job

Despite my exhaustion, I slept poorly, leaning against my pillow and watching the hours tick by. I'm not designed for sleep, it seems. Always too many thoughts chasing each other through my head. One a.m. Two a.m. I finally tossed back the covers at 3:00 a.m. and slipped out of bed. As I paced the apartment at that heartless hour of the night, I was reminded of how I had been unable to adjust my body clock to the demands of the night shift and detested the compulsory rotation in the early days of my career working as a staff nurse on Marilyn's unit at Alberta Hospital Edmonton. I'm not normally given to nostalgia, but I was flooded with memories of that unit.

Early in her career, Marilyn was a tall, striking redhead with an easy laugh and a quick temper. But it wasn't her face I saw that night. It was images of our work together. We were at the leading edge of profound changes in psychiatric treatment approaches, having great success with a combination of the newly introduced psychoactive medications that were producing unprecedented and amazing results. On the frontline in a collaborative environment with multiple providers from different regulated professions, we worked together, striving to provide the highest quality care. Our work with patients with the most severe psychiatric illness, who had suffered in silence, who had been feared and shunned, was very demanding. Ours was more than an accident of employment. It was a response to a call to serve.

We trusted each other, backed each other up all the way, and thrived as a tightly-knit team in this environment of high emotional intensity. Our devotion to our patients was primary, and our understanding of complex problems, our complementary skill sets, our unique body of knowledge and extraordinary sensitivity served our commitment to implementing best practice. Our shared thoughts had consequences. Our actions had weight. It helped tremendously that our boss was supportive, authentic, and trustworthy. I remember her sharing her knowledge and experience freely, her Head Nurse title lending her words implicit authority. She was candid, fun-loving, human, and at times angry at what she called the system—the system that kept our position at the bottom of the ladder in pay, benefits, and status within the health care system. She was a vocal and passionate advocate for her patients and for better working conditions for her staff. She was demanding but fair. We could count on her giving us feedback without coming across as critical or judgemental. She was my most vocal cheerleader, my mentor long before mentoring was recognized as a valued component of leadership. Her influence was woven into my professional development, and her love a constant in my ever-changing world. She encouraged me to dream big, and as a 20-year-old, new in my profession, I looked up to her as her strong hand helped to launch me on a professional journey that has been anything but predictable.

Throughout my career, I retained as a guidepost the feature that defined her most in my head: the tenderness she demonstrated for those struggling with mental illness, those forgotten and over-looked; those negatively stereotyped and labelled by society as crazy people. As the years passed, we often shared our distress at the slow progress in the field and at the stigma that continues to keep people away from the help they need. We celebrated the spectacular triumphs achieved by medical science with acute medical conditions but mourned the lack of similar success with mental health interventions, leaving in place a system that still often fails to provide required medical services and protection for vulnerable people with mental illness.

"We can do better," she'd say. "A lot better."

"I couldn't agree more," I'd say. "A step forward is not enough. We need a giant leap, and it doesn't seem to be forthcoming."

I followed in her footsteps with the grit of a warrior, devoting my career in mental health of close to fifty years of service and advocacy.

And it wasn't all about work. She participated joyfully in our social activities. One of our favourite things was to gather at our colleague Emma's home after a particularly tough series of shifts. Emma was the chef among us. She was famous for her pineapple cheesecake, a recipe she'd brought with her from Poland. She's long gone now, but I still have her recipe and I see her face every time I make it.

As I reminisced, it struck me like a punch in the belly that with Marilyn's passing, I had lost the last witness to this part of my professional journey, our shared history. I feared this meant the history itself, with no one left who had held my hand walking through it, was now erased. I didn't want it to be that way. I felt bereft. I also worried that with no obit, no eulogy with a sound picture of her life, her grandchildren wouldn't have the opportunity to know and to contemplate the importance of their grandmother's history, a part of her story she held close to her heart.

I fixed a cup of chamomile tea. Pulling a tea bag from a box with the bold label "Celestial Seasonings" gave me a moment of wry amusement. I then shuffled around the apartment for a while, drawing comfort from the warmth of Marilyn's china teacup and the surprisingly profound silence stretched across the suite. Something I had observed living in this large apartment complex was that activity of some kind and noise were ever present. Not so right now. I could hear, rattling in my head, all the thoughts I would have preferred to avoid.

By morning I had achieved a few hours of restful sleep and had regained some emotional equilibrium, a fresh resolve, and the strength needed for the challenges of the day. Still in bed, I reflected on the tasks to be completed. While I had taken care of Marilyn's apartment over the last few days, as her friend and according to our understanding, my authority to make decisions as Executor officially and legally began as of Marilyn's moment of death. *It's show time*, I thought, *time for me to carry out her will's instructions.* With my recently acquired Executor savvy, I knew that my first responsibility, after securing the assets, was looking after the funeral arrangements. The law is clear on this—the Executor has the last word on funeral decisions. And the reality is that the funeral brings forward for the Executor the first and immediate liability. I felt the need to be careful and thorough.

I also knew that I would now have to draw on a diverse set of skills to deal with the range of complexities, from legal, accounting, banking and tax matters to the more mundane tasks associated with the disposition of the apartment contents. The call to channel my emotions such that I could engage in the uniquely creative process required to complete these tasks under the full weight of my grief, I realized, was the price of admission to the Executor role. I would not be deterred.

The law would not allow me to delegate my decision-making responsibility for any of these tasks. Once accepted, the role provides no opportunity to pass the buck to anyone, I mumbled somberly, and every step the Executor takes in the process of implementing the will's directions leaves a trail of breadcrumbs that can be traced right back to her. I appreciated that I didn't have to do this alone, however. Having a team, as in any major undertaking, is critical to success in navigating the process. Many hands make light work, as my friend Vern often says. So I intended to bring Michael along with me every step of the way for several reasons.

1. He had indicated a desire to learn.

2. He wanted to help and had taken the whole week off work to do so.

3. I believed that participating in this process would help to alleviate the guilt he struggled with and would hopefully lead to a healing of old wounds, providing solace in his grief.

4. He was smart and had a great sense of humour; he was a hard worker and a delight to work with.

5. He was a solid driver. Once again, I had a chauffeur.

6. This time I wasn't concerned about being dependent. My motivation was to take every measure to minimize the costs associated with the management of the estate, thereby leaving as much cash as possible in the pockets of the beneficiaries. Michael and I would consult as a team. There would be no secrets. I would take him under my wing and make it worth his while.

Still in bed but unable to rest, the perfectionist in me was vocal: no time to wallow in the morass of your bereavement, was the nagging message.

I could hear Head Nurse Marilyn's admonishments: "Come on," she'd say. "Waiting to be in the mood is a luxury you can't afford. When there's work to be done you get up; you get to work. And if you're lucky, the mood will come and find you."

I could hear her voice, her expressions, her direction, all so evocative of who she was at the time of the remembering.

Hers was one of the voices behind my deliberate efforts to develop proficiency in managing my emotions. Over time and with practice, augmented by professional training, I had learned to channel my energy into thinking, reflecting, taking action. Some people I know thrive on confusion, but that's not me. I had become a woman of details, not compulsive but meticulous. I couldn't wish away the fact that I had wept like a child crying a river the night before, but today I'd be focused on the job and would be tough.

Everyone who knows me knows I've always been a planner. Here's one of my back stories to illustrate the point, and I promise you it hasn't been airbrushed. I told my family when I was in grade four that I would become a nurse—not just any kind of nurse but a psychiatric nurse. This plan was triggered by an event during the annual career week in my rural community school, which housed elementary to grade 12 students. Tables full of booklets and brochures lined the school hallways. These were meant for the older students, and the younger ones were discouraged from messing up the materials. Despite the admonishments to our class to stay away, I sneaked over during recess one day and found an Alberta Hospital brochure promoting their nursing program. Looking over my shoulder and around me like a thief, I hid the brochure in my bag and took it home that day. It was the only thing I saw. The only thing I took was a simple brochure that to my child's mind was abstract, mysterious, and exciting. It lit a fire that defined my calling and sealed my destiny. I protected and nurtured in a single-minded way what began as a child's conviction so that it could not be extinguished, and in 1965 my dream was realized when I was accepted into Alberta Hospital Edmonton's Psychiatric Nursing School.

Over years of practice, I had become a proficient task master, unwilling to surrender my days to random developments. I believed in the value of consecutive tasking, the practice of doing one thing at a time and aiming for quality as opposed to the current popularity of multitasking, which in my view could only result in work of inferior quality. Also, I recorded everything in my journal for review, reflection, and decisions on the next steps. Someday was never my favourite day of the week. I was the person who got things done. This value, modelled by my parents during my formative years when I was no more than an impressionable moppet and they were my heroes, was further reinforced in nursing school to stay with me for life. It was written in my blood, stamped on my skin. I had to live up to my reputation.

While I embraced the fact that no amount of list-making can hold life together, (because I had tested this many times), I knew that a checklist of items for completion would make any job more likely to get done. I'm not talking about a spreadsheet on a computer but a notebook that comes with me everywhere I go. Some people don't appreciate the value of list making, but as I see it, making a list is complexity made simple, an elegant time and energy management system, an optimistic and hopeful practice. It's like spot-focusing so you won't get dizzy and lose your footing. And here's a funny thing—once it's on the page, the list is also imprinted in my head, and I can spend my entire day without ever needing to look at it. The world is friendlier to a person with a plan, as if being prepared is a cosmic way of getting the universe on your side.

I jumped out of bed, got my pen and notepad, and over breakfast and enough coffee to jump-start my grey cells, I made my list for what was my first real day on the job. The items didn't even need to be prioritized. They were all things that must be done to maximize estate revenue by closing the apartment on time. I knew I would need an early start to each day and wanted to hit the ground running—not to hold myself in rigid control but to be rock-steady, and not to deny my grief but to set it aside.

I would be the majestic green ash in my front yard, which when confronted with the loss of a limb doesn't heal but seals. Now was not the time to dwell on death, loss, or feelings. I felt it important, even imperative, to defer these to a later date, to unlock them when the time was right. I wouldn't disappear into the Nether eating-my-heart-out, obsessed, morose. My loss. My feelings. My timeline. My terms. My rules. I wince in retrospect as I write these words, part of me wondering if there's a deep psychology here I will need to address at some point. Should I give myself bonus points for being tough in postponing the grief rituals particular to this life transition, or would there be a price to pay for succeeding at it—a piece of my soul, perhaps? Would I be blindsided at some point by wrenching grief? Maybe. Some days were harder than others.

1. Call Lifeline. Set up an appointment with the volunteer service to pick up the medical emergency alert device and pendant Marilyn wore around her neck.

2. Call the Nurse Next Door service, which provided nursing care for several days from 10:00 p.m. to 6:00 a.m. They need to pick up their binder, which contains a record of the care they provided.

3. Call the Red Cross Health Equipment Loan Program. Set up a time to deliver the cane, walker, and supplies they will gratefully accept.

4. Call the property manager to notify him of my plans to vacate the apartment by the end of the week.

5. Call Patrick for Marilyn's WIFI address and computer password.

6. Begin packing contents of the china cabinet.

7. Call TD Canada Trust for a meeting.

8. Call the accounting firm for a meeting.

9. Take the bag of drugs to the pharmacy for disposal on the way back from the funeral home.

10. Make funeral arrangements.

At 9:00 a.m., I was surprised by a phone call from Marilyn's family doctor, a woman I'd never met. She called to say that she knew about me from her conversations with Marilyn and wanted to express her condolences. Wow! No wonder Marilyn liked her so much.

Patrick then called to say that he had Marilyn's B.C. services card, which I would need for ID purposes. He placed it in the morning mail.

Then it was Melanie's turn to call. Julia had been in touch with her. She would come by tomorrow to discuss the items her church group would accept.

At 10:00 a.m., the director from Springfield Funeral Home called. We settled on a meeting time for 3:00 p.m. He advised me to bring along Marilyn's birth certificate, her will, and her Social Insurance Number.

The day slipped away as, absorbed in my work and silent contemplation, I began the meticulous process of packing up a life, focusing on the contents of the massive china cabinet and keeping sadness in the shadows—sorting, tissue-wrapping, and packing my grief. I handled with kid gloves the collection of exquisite, fragile crystal goblets, each piece a beautifully hand-crafted work of art, catching the light even as they sat on the shelf. Equally precious was the translucent fine bone china set, a service for 12, with all the matching serving pieces. Marilyn had coveted and collected these with a borderline spiritual zeal, at least in the process of their acquisition, planning and saving over years for a complete set. These collections weren't a direct representation of my friend but certainly a part of her identity as a gracious hostess. She had a sense of home, of elegance and tradition.

Her instructions were very specific on which of these treasures, in mint condition, would now be handed down to each of her grandchildren. Would they use these in their homes? Not likely, I thought. In today's world, our kids tend to rent rather than own. They live in smaller homes, and in their relaxed lifestyle with open home designs and no formal dining room, meals are typically served in the kitchen or, in many homes, in front of the television. The young ones aren't likely to break out the fine china and crystal very often, if ever, and the elegant sterling silver flatware set, complete in its baize-lined vintage chest, had probably seen its last polish some time ago. Marilyn had lamented how few were the occasions the table had been set since Richard had died 18 years ago. I'm imagining her having a candle-lit dinner with him now, in some fancy dining room somewhere in the great beyond. Through a sense of loyalty and sentimentality, the kids may find it hard to relinquish these treasures. They won't, but if they were to ask me for advice, I'd say:

"These are exceptionally beautiful collections. Keep them handy. Use them often. Don't wait for a special occasion. Those simply don't come often enough. Enjoy them. Raise a glass to your grandmother every time you use that crystal. Find creative ways to make these gifts your own, to give them a second life in your home. But kiss the collection goodbye if you're not going to use it. Find ways to honour your grandmother through your memories rather than through a box full of delicate china forgotten in a basement corner."

I confess, this process caused me to reflect on the wisdom of a simple unencumbered life, on the futility of accumulating goods some would call expensive dust catchers, even though they add tremendous charm to a room and provide clues on the character of the person who lives there. Why work so hard to buy yet another treasure to be enjoyed temporarily at best, to end up, potentially, in a shop somewhere specializing in dead people's stuff? The market is actually flooded with baby boomer rejects. I've seen the over-flowing shelves at the thrift stores, the local Goodwill and Value Village, evidence that millennials especially are known to reject these hand-me-down family once-upon-a-time treasures—beautiful, expensive, or not.

I understand it. It's not because they think the things we see as beautiful are crap but because, as a group, they tend to spend their money on experiences rather than things. Immersed in our growing digital world, they like to collect digital items rather than physical collections to embellish their home. Believe me, I wasn't sitting in judgement. I have friends who collect shoes, for goodness' sake, or fancy running gear. I collect books and feel fully entitled to do so. And I own beautiful antiques and collectibles I know my kids have absolutely no interest in. I can feel their rejection as I think of my treasures and what will become of them when my day comes. In the middle of these reflections and valuable collections, surrounded by boxes full of fragile crystal stacked floor to ceiling, half-full boxes, crackling tissue, tape guns, tape rolls, and felt pens, all borrowed from Michael, I was inspired by an

Oprah-esque epiphany: my children and grandchildren don't care what I own. They just value my love and attention, a thought that filled me with an inexplicable rush of love.

I know I was reacting in the sadness nestled deep inside my skin and taking little comfort in knowing I wasn't alone. I shrugged off the value of Marilyn's collection, acknowledged that I had been a wanton spender in my youth, and resolved that from that day forward, I wouldn't give my family and friends the burden of another doodad or thingamajig or knick-knack or bric-a-brac of any description. It struck me as I taped the last box from the cabinet that I now felt zero need for shiny things; that perhaps this process had served as a vaccine against consumerism. My new philosophy: If it's not consumable, don't buy it. Or perhaps I would adopt the frugality motto: Use is up, wear it out, make do or do without. Well, I might not go that far.

I was in the zone, and before I knew it, Michael was at the door to pick me up for the appointment at the funeral home. We were met by the funeral director, who, like the undertakers of old, was intent on making the complex language of death clear for us, and the process efficient. He inspired confidence. Marilyn had worked with him in pre-planning her funeral, leaving only a few decisions still to be made.

"Take us through the process steps," I asked him, knowing that death comes with its own set of protocols.

"We've scheduled Marilyn's cremation for Wednesday morning starting at 10:00. We have an on-site crematorium here. That is not an adjunct," he emphasized. "We consider this an essential element in providing continuity. Marilyn's body will be safe here. She will never leave our care until the time comes for the final ceremony.

"The law in British Columbia requires a 48-hour waiting period after time of death before cremation. This allows us to obtain all the necessary authorizations. You have the option to see her body before cremation and to be in attendance for the cremation itself, a six-hour process. I will facilitate that for you if you like."

We both declined. I gave my authorization for cremation and proceeded with the selection of the cremation container, an environmentally friendly, no-frills option. This was truly a place for one-stop-shopping for all of one's funeral needs, a sanitized process to say the least.

Selecting an urn to preserve Marilyn's ashes was next, a somewhat more joyful task than the selection of the cremation container. The choice, out of the extensive collection, seemed immediately obvious to both Michael and I as we spotted a lovely rose cloisonné urn trimmed in gold and with a highly polished wood base—a masterpiece of craftsmanship. Both the colours and the delicate, classy look of timeless elegance reflected what Marilyn had loved in her china, her furniture, the paintings on her walls, her clothing. We gasped at the price tag but agreed that this bit of luxury would, in a small way, celebrate Marilyn's unique personality. We were convinced that she would wholeheartedly approve of this selection. I later sent a photo to Elena and Ana, who agreed it was a perfect choice.

Marilyn wanted no traditional funeral, no memorial service, no eulogy. She had said on more than one occasion that she didn't want anyone to mourn for her.

"Not even an obituary in the local paper," she'd said in a stern voice that brooked no argument. "My family and friends will know I died. No one needs to read about it."

The internment of the ashes was set for Thursday at 3:00 p.m., when Michael and Julia were available as well as Mia and Trevor, who would skip their university classes. Jason would not be able to attend.

The funeral director then confirmed the list of the services the funeral home would provide for us:

a. Registration of Marilyn's death with the province.

b. Cancelling her Care Card, her provincial health insurance coverage, with B.C. Health.

c. Notifying Service Canada for the Canada Pension Plan Death Benefit. Service Canada, he explained, pays a one-time death benefit to the estate of anyone who paid into the CPP during their work life. The Executor has to apply for it, a task, I was happy to hear, that would be completed by the funeral director.

d. Notifying Human Resources Development Canada to cancel Marilyn's Social Insurance Number.

e. Providing me with one original and twelve copies of the death certificate.

    "It may seem like a lot of certificates," he said. "You'll be surprised at how many you'll need as you're dealing with the banks, insurance companies, investment firms, and service providers of various types as you administer the estate."

It's true. I didn't appreciate at the time that the will and the death certificate would become my calling cards.

I agreed to come back the next day to collect the documents and sign a number of legal forms. The meeting was over.

Back home for more packing, I got in the zone once again and was startled by the ringing telephone. It was Jack inviting me over for a wine and a chat. Our visit was short, since Jack, I noticed, was exhausted. Jackie had had a seizure during the night, which had meant little sleep for his father.

Back in the apartment, I slipped into my soft flannel pajamas and went to bed, notebook in hand and checking off items on my list with my highlighter pen. I signed off for the day, satisfied with the page now neon yellow.

7

Tuesday, November 21, 2017

—

Invasion of Privacy

My workday began with the manager of the apartment complex, Thomas, who brought me a sheet of cleaning instructions required for a full refund of the damage deposit. He insisted that we had to take out the washer and dryer, which weren't part of the apartment appliances. We would have preferred to leave them, but no way. He was not receptive. Sometimes you can't even give good stuff away. He assured me we wouldn't have to pay the December rent if we were out by Sunday. I confirmed our plan to be out on Friday, so we set Monday morning at 10:30 for his inspection. He left me a sheet of moving rules and instructions. I felt a bit under the gun but was grateful for tight timelines and days full of tasks that served to reduce the opportunity to anguish over emotional issues.

Today's checklist:

1. Sign documents at the funeral home.

2. Change address at the post office, redirecting Marilyn's mail to me. A hundred bucks will buy this Canada Post service for a full year—a necessary expenditure. Remember to bring along the will and the death certificate.

3. Ask Michael to put the bathroom door back on its hinges and remove the handrail in the bathroom as requested by the apartment manager.

4. Begin sorting through the documents in the filing cabinet to make sense of the financials.

5. Confirm plans with Michael for moving out on Friday.

6. Call Ana about the Morrisseau painting. I imagine she will likely have started the process toward authentication.

7. Make an appointment with Interior Savings to go over the financials and take out the contents of the safety deposit box.

8. Ask Michael to contact his cousin, who has a key to the safety deposit box. He needs to return it to me.

9. Check Marilyn's desk for loyalty rewards cards, which I will need to distribute.

Patrick had done some truly helpful things during his time at Marilyn's, including selling her SUV and paying off and then cancelling her credit cards. It's important to be quick about cancelling credit cards, I've read, because it's not uncommon for fraudsters to take advantage of the information available in the obituaries. I was grateful for the tremendous time and effort his work saved me. He had also helped Marilyn prepare a bank draft for each of her grandchildren while she was still competent to do it. He called to say he had inadvertently taken these home with him but had sent them in the morning's mail.

"Watch for the mail, he said. "These will likely arrive Thursday."

Melanie arrived at 10:30 as did Julia. We loaded Melanie's SUV with all the clothing, shoes, and personal hygiene items. We made many trips up and down two flights of stairs, in and out of the rain to the SUV, until the closets were emptied. Melanie was up and down, in and out, right along with Julia and me, a performance that had us in awe of her extraordinary energy and stamina given the fact that she was 85 years old. And she had short legs. Her gratitude on behalf of her church for all those who would benefit from these gifts was heartwarming.

We then loaded Julia's SUV with boxes of delicate china to take home for Mia and Trevor, who still lived with their parents, and boxes for Jason, which they would store for him until his next visit.

The morning sneaked past us into mid-afternoon when Michael picked me up for the signing formalities at the funeral home and to get the original and copies of the death certificate. The director also gave us a series of booklets on grieving, which I encouraged Michael to read with his family.

Next stop, the post office, where I used the first copy of the death certificate. This was an enjoyable transaction, conducted entirely in French with an engaging young francophone woman who had just moved from Winnipeg to Kelowna.

Back at the apartment, Michael put the bathroom door back on its hinges and removed the safety handrail in the bathroom. We then packed and loaded his SUV with boxes of fragile treasures. Michael and Julia had come to an agreement with the kids to store the apartment contents in their basement and garage for now. It was all very good quality and would be handy when the young ones moved to their own apartments. Jason would collect his items there.

I was hesitant about our timeline of moving out on Friday, worried it would perhaps be perceived as somewhat aggressive by all concerned. I didn't want to be insensitive to the family's feelings, given that this timing was so close to their experience of loss. A Friday departure, however, meant a month's rent money in the kids' bank accounts. Michael and I both felt good about that scenario, thinking there was no specific attachment to the apartment itself. We agreed it could be done. The process was already well underway. We were in sync, kindred spirits, working together as a team like the proverbial well-oiled machine.

"Hey, wait up for a city girl," I protested as Michael rolled ahead with a dolly piled high with boxes.

"You're a slave-driver," he said in a gruff voice and with a look that suggested he had mischief in mind as we began loading the boxes in his vehicle.

"You never stop! Don't you ever need a break? You're as demanding as my boss!"

It was a soft jab, but, like him, I was in the mood to spar.

"It's a gift!" I said, feeling a tug of pure, simple mischief along with a surge of affection for this big man so obviously committed to being helpful. "Given to me at birth. I'm a woman obsessed with getting the job done. And, Michael, I need someone to boss around. Let me remind you it's count-down time. After today, we only have two days left before Friday's moving deadline. There's a lot to do between now and then, so make your watch your best friend."

I rattled on as I worked to keep up with him: "We're in a sprint, Michael, not a marathon. There's no stopping; we are racing against time. The trick is to keep the rhythm even when we feel like stopping. Think of this as play time…speed play," I cajoled, big grin splitting my face. "You'll see, this approach is a sound one. Notice we're moving fast enough to be in all but two places at once. Yeah!

We just need to white-knuckle it 'til the process is done, a small price to pay to make sure we meet our Friday goal."

"Aha. Aha. Aha," he mocked, stopping in his tracks and staring at me with his big brown eyes and a smile of baffled amusement. "You make good speeches but guess what—your idea of fun is quite different than mine."

"There really is no time to sit on our haunches drinking tea, Mike. Not until Friday night. But then we can unwind and treat ourselves to something nice in our tea. Oh, and by the way, do we have movers lined up for Friday?"

"I take back what I said," he wisecracked, hands on both hips either in defiance or resignation, I'm not sure, and shaking his head. "You're actually much worse than my boss! No movers yet," he snarked, getting into his SUV. "I'm still working on that. But I know a guy. He owns a moving company. Don't worry."

"Michael, you are worth your weight in gold!"

I knew he was jesting, but I saw myself and our goal through his eyes and was filled with gratitude for his warm-hearted goodwill.

"I could never do this without your help. Thanks a bunch."

He couldn't resist a grin, a spontaneous flash of humour that erupted into a full laugh as we waved goodnight. Our banter, it seems, added sizzle to a demanding task.

Julia came at seven with hamburgers and fries. Our conversation over dinner eventually took us to the elephant in the room— the behaviours behind the long seven years of silence, painful stories needing to be unburdened. I appreciated her company, her confidences as we leaned over the table with our latte, and her help with various details. *She is a strong woman*, I decided. *She will be an indispensable ally.*

We finished packing the fragile items for another full load in her SUV, this time including the beautiful paintings, each with the name of the intended recipient marked on the back. Nobody was going home with an empty vehicle. One load at a time, we were getting the job done.

My evening was spent not with Jack, sadly, with whom I had a standing invitation, but sorting through the filing cabinet and organizing personal letters, business correspondence, old bills, outstanding invoices, bank records and document all-sorts in a way that made sense of the financial accounts, the income taxes, and the personal items. This work was much harder than packing boxes. Three hours of uninterrupted concentration over files and every muscle in my body was protesting; my shoulders and my neck especially were screaming for a break. Even worse was the emotional toll of feeling that going through her files was intrusive, an invasion of my friend's privacy, a sensation of trespassing.

I took a break to check my emails and found a message from Ana.

Subject: *Morrisseau Painting*

I have emailed the Art Dealers Association of Canada with the picture attached and asked them for their advice.

Their response: "You may want to contact the Kinsman Robinson Galleries in Toronto. They were the artist's primary dealer from 1989 until his death in 2007 and have an extensive knowledge of his work. They may be able to assist with your request or know someone who could."

Ana would follow up. She was on this!

I went for a brisk walk around the complex and completed a series of stretching exercises. After my nightly check-in at home, a hot shower, and a bitter tonic of chamomile tea and orange rind, I was ready for bed once again with my faithful bed partners—my notebook, pen, and highlighter. I covered the page yellow then started a list for tomorrow:

1. Meeting with TD Canada Trust, Rutland Plaza Branch, 11:00 a.m.

2. Meeting with Interior Savings, 2:00 pm.

3. Call Credential Securities about the registered accounts.

4. Persist with accounting firm contact—no more telephone tag.

5. Confirm moving details with Michael.

6. Update Thomas, who wants to be in the know.

7. Find a shredder. So many old confidential documents I'm not taking with me.

8. Load up Michael's SUV with remaining small items.

9. Call Ana about the Morrisseau painting—missed her call yesterday.

10. Lifeline coming at 12 noon.

11. Book a hotel room for Friday, Saturday, and Sunday.

12. Book a flight home. On second thought, better wait to make sure everything here is done according to plan.

8

—

Undisclosed Wounds

The next morning when the paper delivery arrived, I was at the door to greet my neighbour.

"Jack, I'm up to my eyeballs in sorting confidential documents, and there's a pile for shredding. Do you know where I can get my hands on a shredder?"

"Of course," he said. "I'll be right back."

No sooner asked than done. He was back in a flash with his shredder. "Happy shredding," he said with his usual grin as he headed out the door. I marvelled at how well everything was falling into place. I was away from home but clearly not alone. I had an incredible team, a whole community of friends, working with me on all aspects of the tasks to be done. Nelson Mandela was right in saying, "Those who are ready to join hands can overcome the greatest challenges."

First call of the morning was the funeral director. "The cemetery, which belongs to the city of Kelowna, charges $591.15 to open the niche for placement of the urn and to inscribe the date of death on the plaque. And they require payment in advance.''

Wow, that was a bit of a shock. I thought I was done with cashing out, knowing that the columbarium arrangement was pre-paid and having already paid $4,027 for the cremation services. I say cremation services loosely because this total included a long list of charges—transfer of the deceased, which cost more because it was after regular hours; shelter of the deceased; facilities and equipment; professional fees; office supplies, cremation fee; GST and PST; and the list went on. You get the idea: it's expensive to bury our dead!

Did you know that the average funeral prices have gone up 92% in the last 25 years! Current literature says it's reasonable to project $10,000 for funeral costs. Michael and I agreed in the moment that we'd missed our chance; serving the living by caring for the dead would indeed be a good business to be in. We also agreed that our funeral director had been very helpful and that he, like his colleagues, was seemingly motivated by a desire to help people, not driven by a desire to beef up his bank account. Back on a practical note, we acknowledged the potential that less expensive options might have been available, but we didn't do comparative costing because of Marilyn's instructions to go this route and because what we had in front of us felt absolutely right.

By the way, I learned in my readings that the instructions in the will of a deceased person regarding funeral arrangements are not legally binding on the Executor. I always thought that funeral decisions are the family's responsibility. Wrong. The law actually gives the Executor the right to make funeral arrangements, and that's because the wishes of the deceased, or the family, may in some cases be quite unreasonable and beyond the scope of what's possible given the size of the estate. That law applies regardless of what the will says. Go figure! I was surprised to learn this but not surprised to read that the Executor needs to take care of the payment of the funeral costs as a legitimate estate management expenditure.

But what if I told you another thing in the literature that caught my attention and was an even bigger surprise? Headstones aren't considered part of funeral expenses. I'm sure you'd likely want to know what I'd been smoking lately. What can I say? It's true. The Executor does not have the authority to pay for a grave marker of any kind out of estate funds. The beneficiaries can buy a headstone after the estate is settled or the Executor can get approval from each beneficiary in writing for the purchase of a headstone. So strange! No one wants the grave of their loved one to go unmarked. I wondered who came up with that rule and what the rationale was behind it, but I didn't find the explanation.

None of this was an issue in Marilyn's case. Her choices were so simple and reasonable there was zero cause for concern. In fact, there was ample reason for me to be deeply thankful that she had attended to all the funeral details, leaving me as her Executor with nothing to worry about.

I paid with my credit card, realizing that waiting for the bank to pay for these services would generate a delay I wanted to avoid. I asked the director to bring me a receipt when we gathered for the ceremony the next day. Having receipts and keeping detailed accounts of every transaction is a critical part of my work as Executor. I'll need this for accounting to the beneficiaries and for reimbursement of my already substantial expenses.

The meeting at Canada Trust was brief and productive. Marilyn kept an old account there for the monthly deposits of the pension cheques she received from Germany, a pension that Richard had passed on to her from his employment as a youth in that country. Having all her account access details felt weird, especially the security questions, to which I realized I knew all the answers.

"What is your favourite TV show?" *Little People*

"What is your favourite dessert?" *Vanilla ice cream*

"What is the name of your best friend?" *Elena*

I could easily pass this test.

I deposited the cash I found in Marilyn's wallet and bedroom drawers. Then, on the advice of the account manager, which I really appreciated, I asked to close the account so that all the funds could be consolidated at Interior Savings, where Marilyn did most of her banking. For this to happen, we had to fill out a form called a Waiver of Probate, which was then signed by their manager. The account was closed, and I left with a cheque to deposit at Interior Savings.

Before going to Interior Savings, I believed it would be important to check in with Marilyn's investment advisor at Credential Securities. Luckily, we connected at first call. She confirmed that all of Marilyn's accounts there had been closed recently. The cash account as well as the TFSA and RRIF had been transferred to Interior Savings. The RRIF was reinvested through them. Yeah, one more piece of the puzzle solved. I attributed this consolidation to Patrick's work and sent him silent but heartfelt thanks. Marilyn didn't have a detailed records organizer I could find that would provide a clear account of her personal and financial affairs. I looked for one, since I'd become familiar with a variety of formats in my online research. I would have to rely on the banking records.

The meeting at Interior Savings proved to be the first in a long relationship with Adam, the account manager, who proved to be a very fine and tremendously helpful ally. Michael and I sat shoulder to shoulder across the desk from Adam, prepared to learn from him the financial facts and details. I knew very little about the probate process, but I went to this meeting convinced we could avoid probate, since there was no real estate involved, no underage beneficiaries, and all the financials seemed straightforward. There were no complications like outstanding loans or financial obligations, no short or long-term debts, no line of credit. It actually looked like we might be able to bypass the probate route until we opened the safety deposit box. Adam advised us that in British Columbia, the contents of a safety deposit box can't be released until its items are itemized. We made a list together, and Adam kept a copy for his file. My eyes popped as I saw the contents of the box: a collection of valuable coins and beautiful, expensive pieces of jewellery. Each piece was valued with an enclosed appraisal certificate and labelled with the name of an intended beneficiary. I learned that having those appraisals would make it easy enough to calculate the total value of the jewellery, a requirement for the probate application. Without these, I would have had to reach out to third party professionals to establish their value.

I had seen Richard wear his gold watch, of course, and Marilyn her emerald earrings, but so long ago I'd forgotten. Michael remembered. His sadness became increasing palpable as we took each item out of the box to make a list of the contents. He commented quietly on his memories of certain items and questioned why other pieces weren't included, wondering what had become of them. It was a mystery we wouldn't solve at the moment but I did find the information later on in Marilyn's notes. Given these findings and the overall value of the estate, we weren't allowed to remove the contents of the safety deposit box until probate was achieved. I protested the need for this step, of course, but Adam had the requirement for probate confirmed by his superiors, who were adamant we had to go this route. Nothing to be done, I deposited the cheque from TD Canada Trust into what had become an estate account and was reimbursed for my expenses to date, the large part of which were the funeral costs.

I now needed to find a lawyer. "Not on my to-do list," I grumbled. How would I go about this? The books I read advised a complicated process including activating your network, getting the name of several lawyers, creating a shortlist of three or five, and interviewing them to find someone with the right expertise. And that's not all. Before confirming your selection, you must, according to the advice given, visit the law firm's offices to ascertain a number of factors, including how well you're treated. Gees, following that process would take absolutely all of the time I expected to spend in Kelowna and maybe more. I chose a simpler option that seemed to me obvious and ideal. I surmised that the relationship Marilyn had with her lawyer over the past several years was positive, since she'd used him and no one else, as evident on the documents in her files. I decided David was the one. If his practice included wills, I reasoned, it must also include estate law, which would put him in a very good position to now represent me. The lawyer represents the Executor in her role, I had learned in my readings. He does not represent the heirs or beneficiaries.

I called his office, informed him of his client's death, posed the question on the focus of his practice, which he confirmed, and then requested a meeting with him in the next day or two.

"I'm the Executor," I said with audacious pride. "Please say yes. I'm here to attend to the estate, but I'm going back home to Winnipeg on Monday."

I was in luck. His practice did include wills, estates, and trusts. In fact, he did a lot of estate work. I was relieved to hear him say: "Sure. Friday at 2:00 p.m. Bring the will, the original death certificate, the bank information, and expenses incurred to date. I look forward to meeting you."

Now for accounting. The advice on the process of selecting an accounting firm is the same as for a lawyer, but in my view, the simpler and obvious selection process is the right and best one. I called the firm that had looked after Marilyn's taxes for several years. I can't tell you how many times I patted myself on the back for this great decision, since Irene, who answered the phone, proved to be another tremendously helpful member of my team over the next several months.

"No need to meet now," she confirmed. "Let's talk when it's time to prepare the tax submission for 2017, but don't hesitate to call in the meantime if you have a question for us."

Done!

Michael stopped by for a surprise sushi run for dinner and confirmation of the movers arriving at 10:00 a.m. on Friday. Fantastic! Everything was lining up so beautifully, like a great piece of orchestrated music.

One last task before dinner: my hotel reservation confirmed at the Ramada Inn.

A quick break and then back to the files for a marathon sorting. There was much to do still between this and the cup of herbal tea I planned to pamper myself with at bedtime. At home in a world of logic and order, I felt eager as I cautiously pulled open the first drawer of the filling cabinet and picked up one file, two files, six files more. I pored over the financial records and various statements, looking for evidence of debts owing and was happy to see none. I found solace in the methodical process of discovering, of ordering, of classifying and embraced working in solitude as a fact of life for me in this role. I was my own companion, for better or for worse, firing on all cylinders with a mission to finish clearing out the den that night, and that included not only the filing cabinet but also the deep desk drawers. I found a large pink floral zippered bag in the closet and was determined to fit in it all the documents important to take with me. Perhaps it would need to be a bottomless bag, like Mary Poppins', I mused. In went the required seven years of tax returns, financial accounts, and a variety of other important documents I might need to refer to. A separate pile was for utilities and services I still needed to attend to before the end of the day Friday.

And now the personal materials, I thought, pressing fingers to my tired eyes and choosing to ignore the weariness beginning to take over. Marilyn's life's trajectory was in these files, from her birth

certificate to her high school graduation, nursing school graduation, promotion to Head Nurse, establishment of her private business looking after people with mental illness in Kelowna, and her
later work in long term care. I found her performance reviews,
highlighting her qualities: good communicator, creative problem
solver, collaborative, great skills in time management. There was
recognition of her volunteer work, and letters of glowing reference
attesting to the excellence of her work:

"Marilyn's work is exemplary, a great asset to our community."

I felt proud to see her contributions so nicely recognized in
those files.

In this role, the Executor is forced to take a walk in the shoes of
the person she's lost, to open closets and drawers without knowing
what's inside. You might perhaps think it would be fascinating to
see how people live their life during their private hours away from
the eyes of the world. My own thinking is that this might never be
a safe position to be in. I was struck by the tremendous privilege
it is to sort through the most intimate details of a person's life, a
window into that life no one else has access to. This thought hit me
hard when a single form slipped out of a file in the desk drawer—a
form I had heard about but had never actually seen, so it rang no
alarm bells until I read it in full, twice, to absorb what it meant for
my friend. To say I was surprised would be the understatement of
the year.

I was flabbergasted.

Marilyn had often talked about her enjoyment of casinos. She
participated in organized casino tours with friends that included
choice accommodation and shopping expeditions along the way.
She had amusing stories to tell about both the gambling and the
shopping, but it seems that the gambling became a problem,
as evidenced by the form I found: a Voluntary Self-Exclusion
Agreement with the British Columbia Lottery Corporation. This
form had the effect of her being refused entry to B.C. gaming

facilities. Signing this form is a serious step. The agreement cannot be withdrawn before the expiry date and is followed by a formal and very intimidating Notice of Prohibition forbidding entry to gaming facilities in British Columbia.

She signed this form a year before her death. Clearly she had the courage to face up to a problem, but what a struggle it must have been to come to this point. I searched my memory for something she might have said, something I might have missed or overlooked, a confidence I misinterpreted, a hint, a clue. But all I could think of were ordinary, everyday conversations. I didn't know how to square this away with the confidences we'd exchanged over years of friendship. Surely sharing this confidence would have fallen well within the nature and trust of our long-term relationship. I knew she'd been profoundly lonely the last few years and wondered if that was part of the problem. Protecting this secret, curled into herself like a wounded animal, must have been a tremendous burden, a gravitational pull on her entire being. I'm sure I could read her thinking: *Don't let them know your weaknesses.*

I tried not to sigh but failed miserably. Mystified and dispirited, I wished I had found this form with a note attached—you know, one of those "By the time you read this, I'll be dead, and I won't care" messages that would help me understand what had happened. Why didn't she tell me? Was she afraid I would judge her harshly, that I would define her by this hardship? Was I not a good enough friend? Does anyone reveal the whole truth about themselves to their close friends? Maybe especially not to their close friends. Had she confided in Elena? I pulled myself sharply back from the demon doubts of my adequacy as a friend and from what I realized was unproductive speculation, feeling heartbroken to see that even with her training and years of practise in mental health she had been trapped inside her obsession and unable to find a way to be open about this health problem.

As I mulled this over, it occurred to me that in her time as a practising mental health nurse, addictions were judged harshly, not as a health issue but as a personal failure. The stigma attached to those addictions often drove people to go undercover, and it was a stigma that permeated well beyond the medical system into all aspects of society. Alcoholics were drunks. Drug addicts were bums. Gamblers were irresponsible. We heard little about other forms of addictions, but all were relegated to a life of shame. I knew that people with addictions are everywhere. In our workplace. In our neighbourhood. In our network of family and friends. We might not recognize them, but their presence is real. I knew all this and still I was shocked at my findings. Marilyn's time in the workplace preceded the integration of addictions into the portfolio of mental health, with a focus on empathy and treatment. Alone, in her loneliness, she had not received the support she needed.

The more I discovered in this process of getting to ground truth, the less I felt I really knew her. "I'm not the Marilyn you knew" was the six-word story that rang in my head.

Was I mourning a stranger? I was haunted by how little we may really know about the people we feel close to: the skeletons ready to pounce out of the closets; the parts kept hidden in fear they will be unacceptable, even to ourselves, never mind to those we love; the shadow side that reveals itself in plain envelopes hidden deep in desk drawers or filing cabinets, threatening to take over our whole being even though it's only a small part of our story. The unknown human journey sticks with me in the aftermath. Is anyone ever who they seem to be? Is it human nature to bury our secrets? Death had prevailed. I would never know the details of what had happened, but I now had to accept the irrefutable fact of her addiction. Then it hit me. With this realization, I finally understood the root of the issues and the estrangement between her and Michael and Julia.

My day that had begun with a feeling of great accomplishment had suddenly taken on a grim veneer. Stumbling across this undisclosed wound was deeply distressing. I left my work in the den unfinished, letting the tide of emotions rush through me. I can usually exist in my own company for days in quiet contentment, but now, for the first time since my arrival in Kelowna, I wished I wasn't alone. I wanted to talk about all this, to be stroked, to know that someone understood, but I couldn't work up the energy to reach out for my end-of-day, every day call. This would be yet another solitary bedtime in Kelowna with no one to share in my distress, no one around to offer solace. Unable to shake off the mood, I dragged my feet to bed—a very sad sack. No tea. No calls. No notebook. No pens. I would pray for understanding, give myself a pep talk, and be as strong as I need to be. Tomorrow.

9

Thursday, November 23, 2017

—

Amazing Grace

There was no period of waking that morning. I was just fully awake. "Tough night," I moaned, desperately wanting to stay in my warm bed, eyes closed and a blanket over my head, hoping that sleep would find me again and yesterday would go away. I had to push my grief aside as if it had the physical presence of an unwelcome companion aggressively demanding constant attention, a persistent hum in my ear. "Take the day off," he taunted with a wicked dark smile. "Who do you think you are taking on these tasks today? You might do a better job if you took a break."

I could feel him in my muscles, my joints, my body, my mind, my soul, so I decided to face the battle at all these levels. "Leave me alone," I asserted in a voice that brooked no argument. "Beat it. Let me do my work in peace." The admonishment worked, and strengthened by a sense of purpose and resolve, I kicked my legs free of the tangled sheets, dressed quickly in yesterday's sweatpants and a clean t-shirt, and reached for my precious notebook to outline the day's tasks:

1. Finish sorting and emptying the den.

2. Pack kitchen cupboards and pantry.

3. Internment of Marilyn's ashes 3:00 p.m.

4. Reading of the will.

5. Dinner with Michael and his family.

6. Fill the SUVs for the ride home.

My singular focus on the tasks helped me calm my emotions and achieve a sense of equilibrium. No more surprises in the den. One more room done, boxes ready to move. I carefully labelled blue bins full of a lifetime of treasured photographs. I filled boxes of pantry staples with a long shelf life for Julia to take home and methodically emptied kitchen cupboards, wrapping bowls, pots and pans, vases, you-name-it with Kelowna newspaper pages until I was black to my elbows with newsprint. This painstaking, slow process of packing a life tricked my mind into delay mode, distancing myself from my feelings with a purposeful distraction.

Michael came to pick me up for the internment of Marilyn's ashes just before three. We were only a few minutes from the Kelowna Memorial Park Cemetery located in a historical area of Kelowna—a beautiful, serene, park-like setting with 50 picturesque acres at the base of Dilworth Mountain and across from the Kelowna Golf and Country Club. The thought that crossed my mind: *For anyone who thinks graveyards are creepy, this one would change their mind.* While it's a place that elicits sorrow, it also invites togetherness and serves as an enviable place to rest. And maybe you can skip out to play golf when no one is looking.

The cemetery is indeed beautiful and quite unique. Its design includes the Bennett Memorial Columbaria, named in honour of former B.C. Premier W.A.C. Bennett and his wife, May, with above ground granite monuments for the internment of cremated remains.

It was a cool but glorious autumn afternoon with no wind and an unexpected beautiful bright sun after a morning of pouring rain. Grateful for this, we met Julia, Mia, and Trevor in the parking lot and proceeded together along a brick pathway to the columbarium site. This large columbarium denotes peace, a tranquil refuge, a place designed to honour life and death. I'm not sure I'd choose it over the option of an underground condo, granted far below the sun, but sheltered with no exposure to the elements.

The cemetery seemed to be divided into neighbourhoods. I thought the columbaria, a row of silhouettes standing above the flat headstones and against the background of the golf course, were striking in their elegance. With their black marble fronts and brass engravings of names, I figured they could realistically boast high property values. Who are these people, now Marilyn and Richard's next-door neighbours? My active imagination launched me into their potential stories, their life achievements surely marked by heroic actions and now housed in these tiny condos. What were their careers, hobbies, passions? Did they have a family? Did they have regrets they wouldn't speak about? Decidedly no place here for villains. Each niche is decorated with a laurel wreath of gilded brass. I wondered if this wreath was a symbol of triumph over life's challenges, a celebration of life's successes, a symbol of service. Did it mean those interned here could now rest on their laurels? Another mystery with no answers. Maybe all of the above.

The funeral director stood a respectful distance from where we needed to be. Marilyn's urn rested on a high, round, cocktail-style table by the open niche—the ultimate empty nest, I thought, waiting for its occupant to arrive. Each niche accommodated two urns, with Marilyn's to be placed next to Richard's. As I saw his urn, a pernicious earworm in the form of Andrew Marvell's voice invaded my mind and stuck in a loop like an echo:

"The grave's a fine and private place,

But none, I think, do there embrace."

I caught myself and shook my head, recognizing that despite what logic might dictate, periods of intense grief have been known to send my brain in unexpected wanderings. Irreverence is not my M.O. *Dignity is required here*, I thought in silent self-reprimand, *not tomfoolery*. I wanted the voice in my head to be quiet for a moment, feeling at once grateful no one knew what was going on in my active imagination and ashamed of myself as the powerful lyrics of *Amazing Grace* broke the intrusive echo. The director was playing traditional hymns as we stood in silence by the niche, each lost in our own thoughts, attempting to retrieve some meaning from the experience in front of us, to find the sacredness in the unfolding drama.

Funerals can be a harrowing experience for everyone involved, from planning the details under tremendous time pressure when family members are under a great deal of physical and emotional stress, to making arrangements, sometimes complicated, for attending the event. This funeral was simple, however, with virtually no burden imposed on those of us left behind. Marilyn rejected what she called the pomp and circumstance of traditional, elaborate funerals. She'd laugh and say, "Those are great for royalty, not for me."

Respectful of her wishes, we had no planned graveside service. No memorial service. No eulogy to speak of her multiple personalities, to highlight her unique contributions. No shiny words. Just a simple personal and private affair to suit the family's availability. Regardless, there was a feeling of ceremony, of occasion, of meaning, of sacredness, enhanced by the background music that had the effect of connecting our little gathering to a broader community. The somber clothing we all wore, a concession to the solemnity of the occasion, served as a synchronized show of respect for the woman we loved. Clearly, we felt the enormity of loss shoulder to shoulder in that front row facing the columbarium. I shared the family's sorrow—not the pain of strangers, but theirs and mine together.

Julia, Trevor, and I said a few words of gratitude for Marilyn's rich contribution to our lives and to our community. Mia was unable to speak, silenced by the tears flowing down her cheeks. I glanced at Michael. He stood still, his shoulders sagging, his expression solemn, his eyes those of a man in deep distress. I thought I had a firm grip on my own emotions. It was only when my vision blurred in a moment of pure sadness that I realized I was praying an inarticulate, silent prayer for Marilyn's soul to be at peace. After a moment, Trevor and Mia took the lovely rose cloisonné urn and together placed it for its final rest in the niche next to Richard's. Perhaps he was saying, "Welcome home, at last." A touching image that lingers in my mind. I often think in images and love to play with poetry with my children. I especially like the Haiku format for its balance and grace, for its few simple words with the power to create an emotion. The Haiku in my head as I stood there:

The niche is open
The ultimate empty nest
Welcome home at last

We concluded the brief service with a photo shoot. We didn't linger but quietly headed down the path to the parking lot, leaving the director behind to close the niche.

Michael took a left turn out of the parking lot, his hands a tight grip on the steering wheel.

I looked in the rear-view mirror, my eyes fixed on the graveyard in the glass.

And then we took the exit and left my friend behind.
For this other place and time.

* * *

We had set the scene for the reading of the will to take place at the apartment following the internment of the ashes. Trevor and Mia had taken the day off classes, and Jason was to join us by teleconference. Julia had stopped at Starbucks for everyone's favourite drink, because even people in mourning, or maybe especially people in mourning, need a good coffee. She was distributing these as we all took our positions in the comfort of Marilyn's living room. I pulled up the pink wing chair closer to the couch and to the phone connection, the effect of which was that we all sat in a tight circle. A picture flashed in my mind: my grandchildren's "circle time," their favourite, magical time in the classroom when they all sit in a circle and the teacher speaks words of bonding, gives instructions, and reads them books. It seemed appropriate. It truly was circle time. I even expected to hear a crisscross applesauce.

I was tempted to call on my inner drama queen for this task, making a show of it, a bit of flair for the part, just like you'd see in the movies. But there simply was no drama. Just a very simple will. None of them had seen the will, nor did they have a right to, I reflected. While some families share the will with those who will become beneficiaries, many families keep the will close to their chest as a very private thing. I believe it's useful, important actually, in most instances to share the will with your beneficiaries and to give them a copy. Many of the people I know aren't comfortable with this exchange, invariably leading to worries and concerns that, in my view, could be alleviated with a simple conversation.

The mood was subdued, and silence prevailed as I distributed a copy of the will to everyone in the room while Jason joined us on speaker phone. I saw some fidgeting with the coffee cup sleeves and wondered if they were nervous anticipating the contents of the will. I had prepared Michael and Julia in advance, since the will bypassed both sons and left the assets entirely to the three grandchildren. I wanted them to know what was coming before I dropped the hammer. I read the will, uninterrupted, slowly and clearly, making sure Jason was hearing every word. Everyone remained very composed throughout the reading, keeping their emotions close to their chest. If the kids were concerned that their fathers weren't included in the will, there was no indication. Perhaps they had been prepared or they were simply not surprised given the long separation. There were no questions, just a heavy silence.

I paused a moment for a long swallow of my smooth, luxurious latte and then distributed to Mia and Trevor the envelope Marilyn had left for them and informed Jason of the contents: a bank draft for several thousand dollars, enough to have a very significant impact on their lives. These would certainly not be young adults with heavy student loans to pay back years after graduation. The three of them were simply blown away, left speechless, by this gift. Marilyn had left plenty of love behind—the only legacy, really, that has the power to endure beyond her lifetime. She had left them a tremendous financial legacy, potentially as long-lasting as the hard-wearing fabric made of woven strands of green wool lining her silverware chest. Can anything good come out of the death of someone you love? Well, this legacy, if they used it wisely, would become the foundation for their future success and financial security. The support for their education alone could have a positive impact on generations to come. That's the future right there, I thought, happy to have had a hand in it.

Knowing them as responsible youth, I couldn't visualize the money running like water through their fingers. Still, I felt obliged, knowing that a few sincere words can sometimes inspire a life's direction, to urge them to honour their grandmother's legacy through wise investments. I encouraged them to seek expert advice, and they assured me they would. I thought of giving them a copy of David Chilton's *Wealthy Barber* as required reading, but this perhaps was not the best time. Going through this process for Marilyn and on their behalf, I felt a sense of ownership, perhaps unwarranted. I wanted them to become "The Richest Man in Babylon." The punch line was, I knew, that the long-term impact of her legacy wouldn't be evident for decades, but I also knew that five years, ten years from now I'd yearn to touch base with them just to see how they're doing. *I hope their dreams will come true*, I thought, as Doris Day's voice rang through my head:

"Que sera sera. Whatever will be, will be
The future's not ours to see
Que sera, sera"

"Please be very careful with my envelope," cautioned Jason, pulling me out of my brief daydream. We made a deal. I promised him I would send it by registered mail. We could then track it, expecting it to arrive mid-week the following week. He would notify me when it arrived.

Michael, in his generosity, invited us all to dinner at Brown's, a new restaurant in the neighbourhood. This was important to him, I think, not only because he was a gracious host but because dining together was at the heart of our relationship with his mother. So many meals we enjoyed over the years, stuffing ourselves with Marilyn's famous saffron rice, gingered ribs, baked red cabbage, pepper steak, cheesecake, and freshly picked fruit from the local orchards as we talked with our mouths full, sharing stories, interrupting each other, and laughing out loud at our jokes and the kids' antics. A happy family at the dinner table.

The restaurant was crowded and the atmosphere thick with the smell of good food and wine. Our table was ready when we got there. We had excellent service with attentive and friendly staff. The modern, open design made it busy and noisy, which we might have minded another day. That evening, however, we enjoyed the lively ambiance, absorbing the energy of the place, perhaps an unexpected panacea after the events of our day. As the music blared from the overhead speakers, we kept the conversation on easy, superficial grounds. No one spoke about the funeral or the will. Perhaps it was simply too fresh or too hard or not appropriate within this culture, or maybe there was nothing to say on the subject.

I had a quick flash of my own family's post-funeral meals. These were never quiet, dignified affairs. My siblings and I would all talk at once, if not about the funeral itself then with colourful stories of community events or the people we know—a raucous medley of French and English, facial expressions as punctuation marks, a raised eyebrow, a roll of the eyes, hand gestures, jokes and funny interjections, voice-over-voice, all of us interrupting each other with no qualms whatsoever. Interrupting is not rude in my family. It's a practice made of love, of interest, of comfort with each other. It gave me such pleasure to look back and remember. I found myself warmed and utterly happy with the memory of those boisterous, happy, intimate exchanges—the interaction and byplay exclusive to big families. And a family, unique by almost any of today's standards, couldn't get much bigger than mine without bursting at the seams.

No matter the circumstances, socializing over dinner is good for the weary soul. Our drinks and meals came quickly. We raised a toast to Marilyn and dug in. My potato-encrusted sole in a dill cream sauce, served with rice and mixed vegetables and paired with a local Riesling, my very favourite wine, was delicious. We all agreed our meals were top notch as we chatted, straining to hear each other over the loud music and the voices of other diners, their table talk a backdrop to our own tentative give-and-take. I kept uncharacteristically quiet, enjoying the stories of the trials and tribulations of university studies and summer jobs. It was an excellent way to end an emotional day for five companions struggling in their own way through a painful journey.

Back at the apartment, we had two vehicles to work with. We loaded the TVs and the huddle of boxes stacked floor to ceiling in the closet by the front door; the carefully labelled and annotated ones I had watched Marilyn pack. I also entrusted Michael with the Morrisseau painting, holding it carefully like a most delicate treasure, urging him to place it in a safe spot, to guard this potentially very valuable piece of art with his life, tongue-in-cheek.

As a parting gift, the kids surprised me with two thoughtfully selected keepsakes. The first was a beautiful vintage Birks Quartz mantle clock, which they knew was my favourite item in Marilyn's home. We often joked on my visits that this clock was responsible for the days flying by so quickly, and I'd have to leave in what Marilyn invariably proclaimed was as soon as I got there. I love to see it now sitting on my own mantle.

The second item was Marilyn's Alberta Hospital Edmonton class ring. It's a beautiful gold ring, not big and gaudy like some class rings, but a delicate oval with the AHE logo on a black background, and the letters AHE above the Alberta provincial emblem. Class rings were a very popular piece of personalized bling in the 60s, and I remember really wanting one. I wanted this symbol of my pride in having become a full-fledged psychiatric nurse, a symbol of the treasured memories of my program, the mark of membership in an exclusive club. But these rings were expensive in 1968, and I couldn't afford one. This one fits my ring finger perfectly, and as a youth I would have worn it with pride, but I don't know now if I'll ever wear it. Still, it sits among my treasures, and when I take it out occasionally, I'm brought back to highlights of those days, including the memories I shared with

Marilyn. I melted, unabashedly, at these thoughtful gifts, feeling recompensed beyond measure for my work on their behalf.

I felt good about our day but suddenly quite exhausted. I knocked on Jack's door for a quick gab about the high points of our day and mostly to check-up on him. Then I pulled together the documents, the financials, including the itemized expenditures, I needed to bring to the next day's meeting with the lawyer. I called home, comforted to know everything there was going well. I booked my flight for Monday and signed off, grateful for another day gone as well as it possibly could in these circumstances—another small victory toward the finish line. Tomorrow's to-dos:

1. Moving day—expect movers 10:00 a.m.

2. Meeting with lawyer 2:00 p.m.

3. Check in at the hotel after meeting.

4. Relax.

10

—

Probate

Morning was not my friend, but I got up early to get a jump start on the day. Time had seemed to speed up, with full days disappearing in the blink of an eye as we got closer to the end of the week. That morning the two moving brothers arrived, as expected, at the appointed time. They were tall and brawny with the powerful, broad shoulders you'd expect to see in men who do this work for a living. They were pleasant to work with and very thoughtful, taking meticulous care to protect each item. They had all the tools of the trade to make the process efficient and were done just in time for me to leave for my two o'clock appointment with my lawyer. Michael had been there to supervise their work, face deep in a travel mug of coffee between his instructions and responses to questions. They charged him $400 for this service. I was amazed at what a good deal this was and encouraged Michael to charge it to the estate. It was a legitimate estate management expense, I assured him, and I would make sure he was compensated, but he wouldn't hear of it. This was his personal contribution to the process, as was last night's lovely dinner.

Michael wasn't coming to the lawyer's with me. He needed to be home to receive the delivery and direct the placement of the apartment contents. Julia drove me to the lawyer's office building and went on to do her errands. I reflected on the many places we'd been to in the last few days, but we had really travelled only small distances. All our business was in the downtown area, a few minutes from the apartment and from Michael and Julia's home. Connection was a simple matter with our cell phones always at the ready. The wisdom of not having rented a car was confirmed every day.

David was one of a handful of lawyers in a boutique Kelowna firm committed to providing personalized legal services to individuals and businesses throughout the Okanagan.

I stopped at the top of the stairs for a minute to comb my hair and check my dress. I wanted to put my best face forward, to present not as the imposter out of my depth, the fraud I felt myself to be, but as confident and competent, someone out on important business. *Foolish*, I thought, turning away from the woman in the mirror. *I have nothing to prove to anyone except myself.* I took a deep breath and, shoulders back, walked into the reception room—not with affected nonchalance but with my best totally-in-charge expression. With poise, I introduced myself. The receptionist shook my hand with a "Happy to meet you." It wasn't forced, as if she had to say it, but a candid, friendly welcome.

"Can I get you anything?" she offered. "Tea? Coffee?"

"Oh, no thanks. Don't fuss."

She then excused herself and turned to answer the phone. I had to wait for a bit because I was early. Seeing promptness as a sign of respect, I wasn't just a stickler for punctuality but compulsive about it. I actually detested being late for anything and resented those who were. Maybe I'd loosened my grip a bit on perfectionism since retirement, but it was still consistent with my type A personality to be on time, if not early, for every meeting, regardless of how busy I was. This was good. It gave me a chance to absorb my environment. I was comfortable in this setting and waited with anticipation, reviewing in my mind the questions I needed answered.

My concentration was broken when David came to welcome me and then led the way to his office. I know that first impressions are crucial in any relationship, and I liked David at once—a rare but sure case of trust at first sight. First of all, take my word for it, he had Mr. Nice Guy stamped all over him: beautiful, genuine smile; a face with the clean, shiny look of sincerity; and honesty. No stuffiness about him. He was dressed casually, not as I expected in my familiar stereotype of the classy suit and tie, but I guess as one would expect in the relaxed setting of the Okanagan Valley. He wore designer jeans, leather shoes, a button-down dress shirt, open collar, no tie, no jacket. He came across as bright and knowledgeable, with an impressive vocabulary but no inclination to try to dazzle me with unintelligible jargon. No 12-storey ego in evidence. He was focused on getting the business done without creating pressure by watching the clock. His office also inspired confidence. It was well organized with a clear, uncluttered desk and no stacks of current files creating the risk of a breech in confidentiality. He outlined his fees up front and the basis for charging them. I was immediately at ease and happy to work with him, appreciating that Marilyn's great choice had led me there.

We got straight to work after the most basic introduction. I thought it was strange that he didn't immediately ask for my ID, so I tendered, with remarkable sang-froid, given that I was new at this game, what I anticipated he would request—my driver's license. He said he didn't really need it, explaining that he only needs to feel certain that I'm the person I say I am. And he was certain. Still, he noted the information, probably to humour me.

I gave him my copy of the will, which matched the one he had already pulled from his files. He gave me three copies with his stamp of authentication. I hadn't expected that and wasn't sure yet how I would use them, but I now felt well equipped for whatever lay ahead. He made a copy for himself of the original death certificate I'd brought along.

"Now to the biggest question on my mind: Please explain the probate process to me," I asked, "and why do we need it?"

I had read about probate, of course, as I was gaining familiarity with the language of death. But the word made me squirm with apprehension because it triggered visions of my history as a dental-chair phobic with a fixed idea in my head of a probe being the instrument my dentist uses to dig into the most sensitive spaces around my teeth. A trigger word. A bitter taste. I needed to reach beyond book learning to confirmation through an expert's words.

David explained that we would need to make an application to the Supreme Court of British Columbia for a Grant of Probate. Probate is a hundred-dollar word, a new one in my lexicon, that means much more than the few letters it takes to make up the word. It means proof, with the probate process being a search for proof. In Canada, almost all wills are probated. We needed this Grant because it does four things:

1. It ascertains that the will we have in hand is valid and is, in fact, Marilyn's last will.

2. It formally recognizes me as her Executor with full responsibility to do what her will asks. This means I can move forward with the job without reserve.

3. It gives me as the Executor legal protection I would not otherwise have, for example, protection from complaints should the beneficiaries claim that I didn't handle the estate properly.

4. With a Grant of Probate in my hand, the bank will be comfortable in releasing to me the funds in the estate account and the contents of the safety deposit box without fear of being accused of negligence or misappropriation. They will have the assurance they need that I am lawfully entitled to receive these and won't be open to any risk of giving the assets to the wrong person.

"That might be simplifying it somewhat, but it captures the basics. And you have to be patient in this process," David advised me. "It can take as long as six months to get the Grant, and sometimes longer, depending on how busy the courts are."

He then explained that the application process involved creating an inventory of Marilyn's assets and liabilities, with the value of the assets included in the probate application form. This document is used to determine the probate fees payable to the provincial government, the amount the court will charge for processing the application. Probate fees are interesting. They're a compulsory fee, of course, and the amount you have to pay is based on the value of the estate. David highlighted that the law of wills and estates is provincial law, which means that each province has its own set of rules and regulations. It's important to know this, I thought, when you're working across provinces, as I was with Marilyn's estate.

The formula for the calculation of the probate fees also varies across provinces. I discovered a Canadian Probate Fee Calculator online. Alberta seems to have the best system, at a fixed maximum rate of $400. Ontario has the highest rate, of course. We all know everything is bigger in Ontario. And B.C. is somewhere close, with no fee for an estate under $25,000.00, $6 for every $1,000.00 for an estate between $25,000 and $50,000, and $14 for every $1,000.00 for an estate over $50,000.00. Probate fees are, in effect, a stiff tax on dying, I concluded. Perhaps I should keep silent on this, but in my view, the government could find better ways to generate revenue. Exploiting death surely can't ever be a good practice.

The fact that this conversation about the CRA comes so early in the process of estate management is significant because, as was emphasized for me repeatedly in my Executor work, the CRA always comes first. Taxation debts take first priority over any others, and if the Executor makes the mistake of distributing the estate assets before paying the taxes owing, the Executor will be held personally liable—clearly a pitfall to avoid.

There aren't just good to know but important to know things about what qualifies for probate. For example, life insurance policies, pension plans, and a variety of investments that have one or more designated beneficiaries are not subject to probate fees and go directly to the named beneficiaries. This isn't a cat and mouse game but a reality that clearly underscores the importance of planning your estate wisely so that your money goes to your beneficiaries instead of as a cheque to the CRA. David and I discussed these strategies briefly as we developed the document for the court. I learned that the designation of beneficiaries as an estate planning strategy is perhaps an area that doesn't get enough attention. After all, no one likes to pay more taxes than they have to, nor does anyone desire to spend their hard-earned cash on lawyers and court expenses. Marilyn, I assumed, hadn't received the needed financial advice and hadn't taken these measures, which meant that everything needed to be included in the probate application.

The legal process also involved David notifying the beneficiaries of Marilyn's death, giving them a copy of the will, and advising them that all necessary information had been received regarding the assets and liabilities of the estate and we were now proceeding with applying to the Supreme Court of British Columbia for an estate grant. I had, of course, already shared much of that information, but a formal letter from David would nevertheless go to the three beneficiaries. This same formal letter would also be sent to

Michael and his brother, even though they weren't named in the will. This would give all of them an opportunity, as Marilyn's children and grandchildren, to be heard should they decide to make a claim concerning their interest in or against the estate. They would have six months from the date of the Grant of Probate to file a claim, an application to the court for a share or a greater share of the estate, if they chose this step.

This is another set of strange rules that varies across provinces. In British Columbia, there are a number of ways to contest a will. The court will deem a will to be valid unless someone comes forward with allegations of improper execution, testamentary incapacity, or undue influence—a person who would exercise influence over the will-maker; the grandchildren, for example, in this case. My understanding was that Marilyn was under no obligation to leave anything to her adult children in her will, since neither one was dependent on her for support. A disability preventing either one from being self-sufficient would have created an obligation for support in the will. I believe that rule applies everywhere in Canada.

One of the duties of the Executor is to uphold the validity of the will, another feature of the probate process. I fully appreciated that the potential for someone to contest the will was an important consideration, and that this process created a critical timeline to be careful about. I discussed the process with Michael, and we talked about the likelihood that a claim would come forward. We agreed the odds were small that we would see a claim from any of the family members, including his brother, who had chosen to keep distant from his mother's end-of-life processes.

Over the course of the meeting, David and I talked about Marilyn's story, how she and I had known each other. We reviewed the steps I had taken so far and discussed my plans going forward. Nerves warring with confidence, I asked David if he thought I was on the right track.

He sat back in his chair, shook his head for emphasis, looked at me directly and said, "I'm in awe of what you've accomplished already. Almost 100% of my clients come here in a panic and say, 'I've been named Executor. Now what do I do? Step one, please?' "You've done so much already, and you're well prepared for the rest. I can't quite believe it. Well done!"

I had been seeking assurance from David's expert perspective, worried that my lack of experience was somehow unique. It seemed to me a legitimate worry lurking at the back of my mind. I wasn't fishing for a compliment or affirmation to feed my ego, but his comments reassured me, and the glow from his feedback would last a long time. Yes, indeed! The clients he was referring to would have included me before my research at the start of this journey. So far, so good. In fact, it couldn't get much better.

We shook hands, agreeing to work together by email that weekend to complete the required documents for signature Monday morning. I left his office with a smile on my face and a bounce in my step, and maybe looking a bit the pomme soufflée. Whatever.

Julia was just arriving to pick me up with a plan to drive me to the hotel. I had looked forward to this sojourn as a delightful respite from the grueling pace of the last several days. I thought I was going to shut out the world, catch a few zees. I tried. It didn't work. After an hour in the room I was at sea, in turn pacing and staring out the window at the traffic below. I missed the apartment, where I had been immersed in Marilyn's presence, the company of her scent, her colours, her tastes, her personality, her voice. It had been the command-centre for everything that had taken place. I was drained, having pushed myself emotionally and physically, and felt unwilling to deal with any more issues involving emotions that day, but as it turned out, I also couldn't tolerate being idle in that empty room.

Having nothing pressing on my plate felt like a guilty pleasure, an indulgence I couldn't allow myself; a strange feeling I couldn't shake of being disloyal to my mission. It felt too much like playing hooky. It reminded me of how I felt after finishing the last year of study and exam intensity in my master's degree. It took weeks before I could relax enough to read a novel. Unable to switch off, I made a quick escape to the Orchard Park Shopping Centre across the street, Kelowna's #1 shopping destination and the largest mall in the Okanagan. Browsing would surely be a failsafe way to combat Executor blues. I strolled from one end of the mall to the other, making my way around other browsers and determined shoppers on the hunt for the perfect gift. I skirted around babies in strollers and toddlers with noses glued to the window displays. I drifted in unfocused window shopping, poking through various shops, at one point browsing through a collection of fine kitchen gadgets. I entertained myself with the snippets of conversations I overheard along my route.

"Did you see the price tag on that dress?"

"I'm thinking of one of these for my mother's Christmas stocking."

"My kids would love that fancy robot."

In a creative spin, I expanded on their lines as I walked by, somewhat surprised at every turn by the displays of seasonal celebration: the strings of coloured lights around the shop windows; the Christmas trees laden with colourful, glowing ornaments, one for every taste on the planet; the fat, red-cheeked Santa waiting for the next child to whisper thoughtfully-crafted wish list secrets; the glittering tinsel and garlands here and there and everywhere; the hustle and bustle of the shoppers I saw clearly enjoying their Christmas shopping.

My mind had obviously been elsewhere, and I felt none of the joy of the season. No holiday cheer for me. My heart wasn't in it. I didn't need to buy anything. I just needed to move. In the end, I left the mall not quite empty handed. I bought a lottery ticket. *Gee, maybe I'll win. Slim chance.* I also bought a Jeffery Deaver novel, planning on saving lives and solving atrocious crimes right alongside my favourite brilliant criminologist, Lincoln Rhyme. I considered the unthinkable: eating at the food court as I walked by. It was buzzing with the noisy chitchat of people of all ages waiting in line for their order. I enjoyed the entirely pleasant food smells wafting through the air all around me. The noise and general chaos soon became unbearable, however, and as I motored full speed out of there, I almost mowed down a smart aleck who called out, "Hey, where's the fire?" I opted for some reading time and a later dinner at the hotel lounge, Mickie's Pub.

11

—

Moving Out

I glanced at the clock, not believing my eyes when I saw both hands on nine. A quarter to nine. Yikes! I never sleep that late. *Rise and shine*, rang in my head, a phrase I had used almost daily to get my teenagers out of bed, fed, and to school on time. I saw their youthful faces just behind my eyes and thought of them as adults now, my pride nearly as great as my love for them, the most prized among my life's many gifts. I burrowed under my pillow and bargained for a few more minutes under the covers, but with sheer will and a strong desire for that irresistible cup of coffee, I propelled myself out of bed. I splurged on ordering breakfast in the room and decided this treat would become the order of the day for the long weekend. I ordered toast, cheese, fresh fruit, and coffee and thought of Jack when my order was delivered with the Kelowna paper.

I had things to get done that morning before Julia came to pick me up for the final clearing of the apartment. It was handy that the post office was in the mall across the street. I reached for my ever-present notebook.

1. Mail a policy cancellation request to Capri Insurance. Include a copy of the will and a death certificate, as they've requested.

2. Mail a cancellation of services request to Fortis BC. Include a copy of the will and a death certificate, as they've requested.

3. Cancel Shaw services. Expect a refund.

4. Mail Jason a copy of the will and the bank draft. It will leave on Monday via Express Post and arrive Thursday. Email him the information so he can track it, and let him know his signature will be required when he claims the envelope.

5. Send a photo to my kids of myself taken with the Santa in the hotel lobby reading his "Naughty or Nice" list, proof that Santa has already arrived in B.C. and is now on his way to Calgary and then to Winnipeg. They'd better be good.

6. Finish clearing apartment contents.

Julia arrived as planned and once again handled the driving. We chatted each other up on the way, the happy talk of two mothers proud of their grown-up children and their impressive careers. The apartment was exceptionally clean and our tasks there were simple. We had all agreed that the damage deposit would be used to cover the costs of the required cleaning of windows and blinds and major appliances, and the shampooing of the carpet. We still had to work our magic with a few drawers to clean out as well as the fridge. Ever-resourceful, Jack introduced us to a young woman down the hall, a single mother with a 10-year-old son who was happy to accept the fridge contents. And with that, the task was done. Sadly, the beautiful Mah-jong set with the four-leaf clover were never found. Marilyn must have given them away to someone special.

Back in the loneliness of the hotel room, I had a few hours to organize files and financial documents. As I did the math, the path of the addiction was clear to see. Feeling an acute episode of self-doubt, I questioned my logic and looked for a mistake in my facts, but as I tallied for the third time, I was forced to accept the evidence. Numbers don't lie. It was clear that financials can betray the best kept secrets and that a few behaviours can drive a cascade of changes. "Addiction is a bitch," I proclaimed to the empty room. "A real bitch!" As my sorrow welled up and my thoughts were becoming more than I could bear, I realized the futility of focusing on this lonely process. Eager to brace myself against a return of overwhelming heartache, I went for a long walk in the brisk November air. Feeling more joyful on my way in, I took the selfies I needed with the jolly Santa in the hotel lobby and sent my email. I then stretched my tired body the full length of the fine hotel mattress, finding the usual anticipated escape in my Jeffery Denver.

12

Sunday, November 26, 2017

—

Ripple Effect

It was Grey Cup Day I discovered as I entered Mickie's pub for dinner. The game enthusiasts were at their best, the room packed and alive with their boisterous cheers and groans of dismay. The air carried the yeasty smell of beer; overlaid with the rich aroma of pub fare, it was making me really hungry. I knew the menu from my Friday visit and thought I'd order a Greek salad to take to my room, but to my great surprise, I spotted Jody at a corner table waving me over. She and I had developed the beginnings of a relationship on Friday night. She was the server for my table—tall, slim, and with an evident abundance of healthy energy. I had liked her immediately because of her efficiency and personable forthright manner. Her eyes sparkled in good humour, and I'd observed that her smile along with her banter served her well in engaging clients. She hadn't had a lot of time to spend chatting, but she'd had enough to inquire about where I was from and what I was doing in Kelowna.

"I'm sorry for your loss," she'd said.

Something in the message had caught me a little off guard. It was the unexpected moment of genuine sympathy so genuinely offered against the backdrop of a busy, noisy pub. Her interest had been piqued with my truthful responses to her questions, and when she'd found out I was immersed in managing my friend's estate, she'd kept coming back to my table for more information. I had brought my Deaver book with me to read over dinner, but the book stayed in my bag. I'd enjoyed my marinara and prawns interspersed with conversation bites with Jody in her repeated brief stops at my table. The exchange of confidences hadn't been all one-sided. I'd found out she was a recently-divorced mother of two children, boys ages seven and five. Her eyes shining with pride, she had pulled out their pictures from the wallet hanging at her waist to give me a quick look. On a longer stop she'd confided that she was a nurse who had given up her profession, at least for the time being, to work in this pub.

"What prompted you to do that?" I'd asked, surprised.

"Not an easy decision, but I make better money here. The hours work better for my family, and the work stress level has gone down several notches."

"How is that possible? We need to find ways to nurture and keep our caregivers." She'd nodded her agreement. "I'm also a nurse. Recently retired. We have a lot in common."

As I was paying my bill, she'd asked me to come back for dinner on Sunday. She would join me then so we could talk about wills, if I was willing. I'd said sure, thinking she was just being polite and wouldn't show. But here she was with a great deal of interest, evidently, since she was taking time on her day off for this conversation. I felt a little guilty for having doubted her. I couldn't claim to have well-honed Executor skills, but I had a solid dose of common sense, which I planned to draw on for my conversation with her.

We savoured our wine as we waited for our meal. Jody recommended a Major Allan Merlot from the local Prospect Winery, promoted for its smooth, light finish and subtle flavours of blackberry, red plum, chocolate, vanilla, and rhubarb. I confess the flavours were too subtle for me. I could detect none of them individually, but I didn't care. The wine was delicious, lively, insistent, and with the French paradox hovering at the back of my mind, I vowed to enjoy every sip. It seems a bit surreal in retrospect, but against a background of noisy cheers and boos, we cut straight to the heart of the matter and began a quiet conversation on the fundamentals of all things wills.

"I've never given any thought to making a will, and this topic isn't one that has come up in conversations with my friends. I don't know anything about it, but what you said last night made me think I should be paying attention to this," she said. "Have I just been stupid and missed the boat on this?"

"Don't feel bad, you're in good company. It's an uncomfortable topic because none of us want to think of our mortality, so we choose to ignore or avoid dealing with it. The importance of having a will should be common knowledge, but it's not so common after all. It's surprising, given the extent of our aging population, but the stats show that only one in three Canadian adults have a will. Truly, this is a place in your life where it's important to be proactive."

She looked at me with listening eyes.

"Why is it so important? Is it something I should be making a priority?"

"In my readings, Jody, as I've been preparing for my work as Executor, what I've known for years about wills has become solidified as the first and essential thing we must do to protect our children. Your will ranks high up there as one of the most important documents you'll ever have to sign. I may be overstating the importance, but I don't think so. You have two little boys, so I know you have good reason to be interested in this. Your will protects them in important ways should you die suddenly. Of course none of us like to think about that possibility, but we never know what tomorrow brings, do we? Death happens to all of us at some point. There is no escape route, so we have to plan for that day. It's hard but necessary. Your will includes instructions on who you want to be responsible for looking after your children should you no longer be there for them. That protective impact on children is an important benefit that people often don't realize."

She was intelligent and strong, qualities that flowed through her demeanour as she absorbed the information and formulated her next questions.

"Wouldn't their father look after them? Wouldn't that be the obvious thing to do? Wouldn't it just happen automatically?"

"I don't know your situation, Jody. Maybe that would be the case if you have joint custody, but you might want something different for them. Without a will, your intentions won't be known. It would be important to have a discussion about this with your ex. If he doesn't have legal custody of your boys and you die without a will, then B.C. provincial legislation will kick in. If you don't have your wishes in writing, your wishes won't matter. Too bad. So sad. The Public Trustee will become the guardian for your boys and will manage your assets on their behalf. The court will decide what would be in the best interest of your children, and Child Welfare Services may get involved. This could be a devastating emotional hardship for your boys, as you can imagine. I have a strong feeling you wouldn't want any of that to happen."

She shot me a look that said in no uncertain terms I'd hit the nail on the head.

"It's an unhappy scenario that can be avoided by having you prepare a will with very clear instructions on your wishes for your children's guardianship."

"You're right, this is really important, and I'm sure you'll say there's no time like the present. I'm more than convinced," she said as she crunched her teeth on a crouton she'd been playing with for a while, seeming much more interested in our conversation than in the meal in front of her.

"What else would a will do for me? Narrow this down for me."

"A will is a legal document that directs what you want to see happen with your estate after you die. This would include your decisions about any real estate you might own, and any other property or belongings and investments. This document, also called your last will and testament, becomes official once you've signed it in front of two witnesses, whose signatures will also be required."

I then shared with her the clever one-liner I'd found the week before in the archives of the One-liners Community website: "A will is a dead giveaway." I chuckled as much from her eye-roll and snort of laughter as from the line itself.

"Having a will, however, is no laughing matter."

"I don't own very much, so that can't be very useful in my case," she said with a shrug.

"You might think you don't own much of anything, but I encourage you to make a list of all the things you do own, and I bet you'll be surprised when you total the value. I don't know anything about your finances, but I know you have a home. You might have insurance. You probably have some savings. You might have a favourite possession you'd like to leave for each of your boys. With a will, whatever you own will go where you want to see it go. That's what matters, right? I think you'll agree it shouldn't be left to someone else to decide how your estate is to be managed. Where there's a will, there's a way, as the saying goes. Some people dismiss the importance of a will with the thought that money isn't the most important thing in life. I have children and grandchildren, Jody, so here's what I believe: there are few substitutes for money when you need to house and feed you kids." It was evident that she was getting it. I was not speaking a foreign language.

"I really want to get this done," she said, "but how do I go about it?"

"It takes careful thought and planning, Jody, but the good news is you don't have to struggle with this on your own. There are lawyers who specialize in the area of wills and estates. They know this stuff inside out. You may know one or you many know someone who can give you a referral, or you may want to do some research on the local firms. You may want to call on my lawyer, David. He's great, and I'm sure he'd be happy to work with you. He'll do a good job," I said as I pulled his business card out of my purse and handed it to her.

"What about costs?" she asked as she examined the card and placed it in her wallet. "I hear lawyers, I think dollars."

"I haven't looked into this for some time now, but I think a few hundred dollars would cover the cost of making your will. It's a chunk of cash, I admit, and it might make you think twice about doing it. But it's money well spent. It will be a lasting gift to your children and will give you peace of mind. I think it's common for lawyers to charge a flat fee for this service. Do ask the question when you're doing your research to choose the right lawyer for yourself."

I noticed her tapping her fork against the edge of her plate and heard her thoughts as clearly as if she had spoken: *Isn't there any way I can do this myself with no lawyer involved?* And before she could ask, I added: "You know, Jody, you can purchase a do-it-yourself kit online with templates and samples with step-by-step instructions and discounted prices. You'll even see ads promoting a free will or 'a perfect will for $39.99.' When you look at these, I'm sure you'll be tempted to think it's convenient and a good way to save a few hundred dollars in legal fees. You might feel compelled to choose that route. I was tempted myself, having grown up in a large family with the pioneering philosophy of don't pay someone else to do what you can do yourself. But I don't recommend it, because it's not all clear-cut and easy to put together. So many things can't be addressed with an online tool. I believe it's very helpful in this important process to have someone with expertise help you think through all the implications of your decisions. You deserve to give yourself this gift of peace-of-mind."

"I'm going to make this a priority," she said, nodding in active agreement. "I'm putting it on my calendar for my next days off."

I congratulated her on her commitment and relished the moment, enormously moved by this chance encounter and by the power to make a positive contribution at a time when I least expected to. I had been quite disturbed years ago when I read the stats on the large number of Canadians without a will. I had no time to take up one more thing but had become somewhat fixated on the idea of finding a way to take up the cause. No need. My conversation that evening may have felt like a small thing, an isolated event, but if Jody told a friend who told a friend who told a friend…the ripple effect would surpass anything imaginable. And the telling on this one occasion would become part of a much larger story for the benefit of many children. I asked her to pass on her experience once she'd made her will by bringing the subject of wills into conversations with her friends, highlighting the reasons for their importance. Perhaps her words would land where they were needed, and the personal experience that had meaning for her would help someone else. Mother Theresa once said, "I alone cannot change the world, but I can cast a stone across the waters to create many ripples." Laugh at me if you will, but that day, I was Mother Theresa.

We talked briefly about the role of the Executor, using my current experience as an example of what the role involves. I encouraged her to give some thought as to who she'd like to appoint in this role in preparation for making her will.

"No need to answer this question now, but who can you think of among your loved ones who might be prepared to act on your behalf? That question will also prompt the need for a conversation with someone in your network. It's important to ask their permission before you put their name in your will."

Relaxed. Leaning forward, heads close together like co-conspirators, elbows on the table, we enjoyed the rich tastes and textures on our plate as we chatted about this and that in our personal lives, with funny stories of our kids in the mix. We paid little attention to the game but joined in the cheers for the Calgary Stamps each time the house erupted. It seemed to punctuate the major points of our talk. Too bad they lost the game. We were clearly on the same wavelength, laughing at our own craziness while enjoying a fun and good meal, completely at ease in each other's company. It struck me as we ended our evening with a bear hug that this chance encounter happened at an interesting moment in both our lives.

We might have been long-time friends, so seamlessly choreographed was our evening together. There was an unexpected magic between us. Why this synchronicity? The reason defied logic, and I was forced to appreciate it simply was—we suited each other to a T. That's what's so wonderful about life. It will surprise you if you're open to it. I might have spent the evening in my room with my salad watching TV, and there are many good programs, no doubt. But in doing so, I would have shortchanged myself. Give me the option of time with a machine or time with a human and I'll choose the human every time. This was not a meeting I would easily forget. In fact, I've memorized it feature by colourful feature. Jody gave me her phone number and asked me to contact her on my next visit to Kelowna. I assured her I would love to, but time might not allow. We would have to see.

13

—

A Journey Ends

With a power breakfast under my belt and my bags packed, I was ready for Michael when he arrived to pick me up. We were going to meet with David, with whom I had emailed back and forth over the weekend, to complete the documents necessary to kick-start the probate application process:

An Affidavit of Application for a Grant of Probate. Affidavit, another interesting word, which means a written statement confirmed by oath that can be used as evidence in court.

1. An Affidavit of Assets and Liabilities with the statement of assets and liabilities as Exhibit A.

2. An authorization form giving David the right to receive information on the estate from the bank.

These documents were now ready for my signature. I signed them all with a flourish, using my elegant Mont Blanc ballpoint pen engraved with:

Muttart Fellow
Germaine Dechant

I believe this pen is so beautiful; it adds formality, elegance, and flair to everything I write. I like to use it for all my official signatures. It was a very generous gift, I might say, given to me in recognition of my accomplishments at the end of the fellowship year I was awarded by the Muttart Foundation. A Fellowship year suggests such marvellous possibilities. In my case, it was a sabbatical in which I could undertake a special project of my own design. I chose to use that year to write a book: *Winter's Children, The Emergence of Children's Mental Health Services in Alberta 1905–2005*. I also chose to travel to Europe during that year of flexible time, where I spent six glorious weeks with my daughter visiting the many wonders of Greece, Italy, and France. Each time I take this beautiful pen, this icon of writing culture, out of its case, I think of the incredible gift of that year with pride, joy, and gratitude. Looking back from this distance, I fully appreciate it as one of the highlights of my career.

With these documents completed, my work with David was done for now. I was very grateful for his willingness to work over the weekend, for his thoughtfulness and efficiency, and for seeing me as a Monday morning priority.

From there we had the apartment inspection at 10:30. Anyone who has moved out of an apartment can sympathize with the process. I had checked all the rooms on Saturday and once again as I did the rounds with Thomas, but I left him in the hallway chatting with Michael while I went from room to room one more time. I wasn't being anal, I told myself. I needed to tamp down the nagging worry of having left something behind. Mostly I wanted to say goodbye without a stranger by my side. The rooms were clean, quiet, settled, and almost ready for the next occupants. Thomas was pleased with the spotless suite, assuring us that he had someone for a December 1 occupancy. This was good news, because it meant the estate would be reimbursed for a month's rent, which would not otherwise happen since we had given late notice of our vacancy.

It was time to head to the airport, a quiet drive into the thin stream of Monday morning traffic. We rode in silence for a while, both appreciating the autumn scene. We had no sport or other interest in common to get the conversation going in the midst of weightier matters. The silence didn't feel awkward, and I didn't feel driven to talk just to fill the silence, but I was concerned about this being our last chance for a meaningful exchange before reaching the airport. I decided to break the silence.

"I miss the orchards that used to line this road several years ago. It's a shame that this beautiful orchard land was sold off for commercial developments. We couldn't wait to pick the fresh cherries, and the peaches especially, when we drove here each year with our kids for a much-anticipated summer vacation. And then the highlight would be arriving at your home, where we were so wholeheartedly welcomed and embraced as family."

"Those were special times for all of us," Michael said. "The visits were just never long enough."

Our conversation was extraordinarily soft and slow and tentative. At one point, sensing his distress, I looked at him. He was practically choking the steering wheel and seemed to carry the weight of the world as silent tears rolled down his cheeks unchecked, eyes fixed on the road, a muscle pulsing in his jaw.

"Something's on your mind, Michael. You should just say it."

"I have nobody to blame but myself," he said, fighting the catch in his throat. "I could have done things differently."

"What is it you're blaming yourself for?" I asked the question at the risk of being intrusive, one of at least a dozen more I wanted to ask. I thought it was a simple question, but he was too overcome with emotion to answer.

"There's no point in finding blame, Michael. None of us have a perfect record. It's part of being human. We all have experiences we regret, broken pieces. I've found over the years that our broken pieces inside all rattle a little if you give us a shake. You have to let it go. Don't let these guilt feelings fester. They'll eat you up, you know."

"What's the treatment?" he asked.

I kept silent for a moment, feeling the intensity of his pain and searching for words of pragmatic wisdom. I was deeply concerned seeing in him this level of dejection, which hadn't poked through before in our considerable time together. Every fibre of my being wanted to find a way to ease his mind, to leave him feeling better. I felt regret that this opportunity for sharing should happen just now as we were parting company, running out of time for this serious conversation rendered even more intimate in the confines of the vehicle.

"I think accepting the facts we can't change is really helpful. You're going through a really tough patch, Michael. We both know that grief doesn't happen in a vacuum, and I think you'll back me up when I say you have some important history to sort through."

"What's the use?" he grumbled. "Why bother making the effort?"

"The simple reason is that you want to feel better and get on with your life. I know you're hurting, and it's not easy, Michael, but talk it out. Secrets and shame create pain and suffering. Some things are simply too hard to face alone. Don't hesitate to find a coach, or pour your heart out to a close friend. You might have heard the saying, 'Grief shared is grief diminished.' It's normal to grieve. It's a tough emotion, but it's real. Go see a grief counsellor if you need to. We could all use counselling at times. Getting this off your chest could really help you discover a new way of seeing yourself. Here's the thing, Michael—people change when their perspectives change. You'll feel better when you get this out of your system."

I hoped he would snap out of his dark mood and wondered if he was hearing me as he skillfully manoeuvred our arrival at the airport.

He blinked hard, surfacing from beneath his sadness, and said, "Yes," stretched into several syllables. "I have some serious thinking to do, but thanks to the work we've done together over the last two weeks, I've learned so much and I really want to move forward. I even want to examine my life's work and consider options. I have you to thank for all that."

After our goodbyes and the exchange of wishes for all the best on our respective journeys, I watched him leave with a last wave through the open window. Then I started toward the airport entrance.

My flight to Kelowna now felt like light-years ago. Our whirlwind eleven days together, working as one with our efforts through this emotionally wrenching slog, had been very productive. Funny how you can pack a lifetime in a couple of weeks. We'd juggled the daily details on the to-do lists and pulled it off. The burning relevance of our tasks had served to harmonize our behaviour. As all the pieces fell into place, our long-ago friendship was reignited and strengthened to a place of easy affection. I had given him my trust, support, and appreciation and approached our work together with a high level of collegiality. We were both equally determined to get the job done. He had let me into his life in a very generous way, and we were now seeing the benefits. We were saddened by yet another transition and both appreciated that I would be back within a year to complete the process.

I reflected on my readings about the wisdom of choosing an Executor close to home. Location. Location. Location, the literature says, matters as much in executorship as it does in real estate. There is truth in that advice. I agree it has merit, but I also have come to believe that it may not be as important as it's cracked up to be—at least in this case of a simple estate. Today's ease of travel and our connected world, thanks to advanced technology, would allow me to do almost all the rest of the work from the comfort of my own couch. We don't even have to set foot in a bank these days. Most banking can be done right where we sit. I would rely on my old-fashioned landline as well as my smartphone, email, internet searches, and good old Canada Post. I was anticipating only one more trip to Kelowna at the appropriate time for the final distribution of assets. Bottom line: while it's important to consider location in the selection of the Executor for one's estate, geography doesn't necessarily have to be a limiting factor. In my view, the right personality and skill mix for the job trumps location. In fact, the relationship with the beneficiaries might be more important than linear distance.

As I sat there with these thoughts, I marvelled at today's technology and its personalized high-touch service that makes all things possible. My kids laugh at me for my back-in-the-day stories, but the fact that things have changed radically since I was a youth is undeniable. I'm often in awe of what's possible today, having grown up with no telephone, then with the notorious party line, and then with the telephone attached to a long, winding cord. When I was a young adult, a long-distance call was so expensive, I had to watch the time and make every minute of my call count. There was a time when I'd have to wait a week or longer for a letter to reach its destination. I shook my head and smiled, almost in disbelief at how far we've come and at how many of our social interactions happen online every single day. In fact, it's easy to be consumed by the distractions of cyberspace. And the impact on our children is pervasive. Have you watched our kids with technology and listened to their vocabulary? One day when Zachary was five his mom was looking hi and lo for her purse in the house.

"Zachary, where should I look for my purse?"

Without a pause, he said, "Mom, google it."

Good or bad, do we ever see anybody without a smart phone or tablet at their fingertips today? Don't get me wrong, I'm not up-there on technological know-how, and I'll readily admit that I'm at times overwhelmed by the possibilities. But I'm also not clueless or inept with digital tools. I'm actually pretty tech-savvy for an old lady. Another giggle from my kids when they hear me say that, but I manage. They don't realize that even I know that email is so yesterday. And when I get stuck, those very same kids are tremendous coaches. I appreciate that with today's technology, barriers of old have simply fallen away, giving us the power to do business at the touch of a button and to receive needed information and responses within seconds.

Today's digital age brings forward other concerns, however, for the Executor to manage. It's an important and potentially complicated matter. The Executor needs to be informed of the deceased's online presence and to close online accounts. If ignored, online accounts can appear to be active long after the user's death. This was a simple matter for me in Marilyn's case. She didn't have many digital assets: no social networking accounts, not even the popular Facebook. She didn't shop or do business online. She used email, leaving me with only this account to worry about.

I was acutely aware of my emotions as I sat at my gate indulging in a Starbucks latté after a quick lunch at the White Spot restaurant. I eyed my fellow travellers, absently studying their features and mannerisms, listening to their conversations with half an ear: the complaints, the laughter, the whispers, the stories. Some of them reading, playing with their gadgets, or, like me, distracted and just looking around. My mind was busy soaking up the atmosphere, and I marvelled once more at how stimulating the world of an airport is. The place was teeming with people. It would be a full flight. I watched as they arrived—all ages, sizes, cultures, and types, invariably in casual clothing, a winter jacket over a pair of ubiquitous jeans.

I boarded the plane, stowed my carry-on baggage in the overhead compartment, settled into my seat halfway down the aircraft's cabin watching it fill up from my aisle seat, and buckled up, ignoring the cheerful flight attendants who joked among themselves and engaged passengers with light banter. I closed my eyes and dozed through the flight attendant's safety monologue until I felt the plane suddenly speeding up the runway. Here we go, happy to be heading home.

For once in my travels, I was eager to forego the happy ritual of engaging the person next to me. The last thing I wanted today was an hour-long conversation with a stranger. I had my book on my lap waiting for take-off before the anticipated bliss of getting lost in my murder mystery. Life, however, happens at the airport when you least expect it, and I was soon immersed in a happy exchange with my seat mates as they drew me into their conversation. My fatigue vanishing, I closed my book and stuffed it in my bag. It appeared I would not be returning to it for the duration of this flight.

My companions were two bubbly young women on their way to Dawson Creek—best friends full of happy banter. To our surprise, we discovered that Jeannette, next to me, was my aunt's granddaughter, my cousin. All those clichés about a small world were never more apt! What a fun conversation we had tracing back family roots and giggling over quirky life stories, much to Jeannette's friend's amusement. Jeannette is an entrepreneur, an accomplished photographer with her business established where she lives, in Edmonton. I googled her later on and was happy to see my aunt's face pop up on her website's front page. Made my day!

There is no direct flight from Kelowna to Winnipeg, so I finally got immersed in my murder mystery book while waiting at the Calgary airport. I read all the way home, saving lives, apprehending the villain, and restoring order to the world right along with the forensic genius.

I love that moment at the end of a trip, that wonderful sense of being home. The Winnipeg airport is small, and I saw Bill waiting for me at the baggage carousel. Waiting there is never much fun, but it offered me time to think calmly and quietly while Bill waited for my bag to arrive. Picture this, says my tired brain. Picture this old woman two weeks ago, struggling over a decision, embracing a new challenge, searching for knowledge, and hopping off a plane in British Columbia, not knowing what awaited her. Between then and now she has seen death; mourned the loss of a dear friend; participated in her funeral; conducted the reading of her will; created friendships and allies for a community of support assembled around her; found that doors opened just as she needed them to so that the load was never unbearable; completed an intense marathon of cleaning, sorting, packing, and moving with an incredibly supportive team, all under the pressure of an ambitious timeline; discovered secrets that floored her; worked with banks, an accountant, a lawyer, agents of all kinds; prepared and signed off on official documents; gave advice hoping to help a new friend; bonded with exceptional people everywhere she went; and had what turned out to be, despite the circumstances, a truly amazing adventure, the first part of a journey far better than she could have ever expected.

I am that woman, a fact that sounds strange even to my ears. I am that woman forgetting that fatigue is a physical manifestation of grief, in turn thinking of my small aches and pains followed by: *I have no right to claim I'm tired, given all the support I received from fine people ready, without a second thought, to lend a hand.* I prefer to claim I have learned a whole new vocabulary, the language of death, and a new set of processes. My perseverance prevailed. I understand so much more about what it means to be human. I feel rich with everything I was given, and it's not that I want to wax poetic but that I am overcome with gratitude. I am energized, inspired by people's goodwill and generosity. If everyone behaved this way, I thought, the world would be a very different place—all thoughtfulness and collaboration, a loving sanctuary. I am at times startled, feeling Marilyn's presence giving her nod of approval. If you catch me wiping tears off my face from time to time, don't worry. They're happy tears because I feel blessed…actually, on top of the world.

I am home. My journey is complete. It is over. Fini. The end. Amen.

Whoa! Not so fast, grasshopper. You can be pleased with the progress, but you can't afford to be lulled into complacency. It's really only the beginning. Still, I reflected, it should be all downhill from here.

Phase Two:
The Executor Year

"Opportunities to find deeper powers within ourselves come when life seems most challenging."

—Joseph Campbell

14

—

A New Normal

I landed with a reality check, shivering as I stepped out of the airport. *The winter air in Winnipeg hurts the lungs much more acutely than it does in Kelowna*, I thought, pulling up the collar of my coat, wrapping my scarf more tightly around my neck, and stuffing my ungloved hands deep in my coat pockets. I felt a surge of excitement looking forward to the welcoming feel of my home: the familiar, the routines I'd set up for myself, the closeness of family, and the treasured long spells of solitude. Nothing felt more glorious than the sense of belonging in the world of my own back yard. I was aware that many would label this viewpoint rigid and limiting, while I considered it a blessing, precious comfort; contented with my life precisely as it was.

I absorbed the affectionate silence of my home, also thrilled with the happy awareness that the physical work of my Executor role was done, and I felt enormous satisfaction knowing it was completed in record time. I enjoyed a late dinner and then turned on the TV for the first time in two weeks, prepared to watch an easy romantic comedy. Lying on the couch, however, I realized I had barely enough energy to reach for the remote, so I opted for a very early bedtime in the luxury of my own nest. I should have taken the time to wash my hair, but looking in the mirror, I reasoned that while it was a little oily, it didn't yet look like I'd rubbed it with a pork chop. I could and did choose to be lazy. I felt rather than heard my own sigh as I stretched in my bed, embracing the idea of laziness as its own reward. Nothing seemed more glorious than this after days of rising early to put in a busy day's work. I settled with a sense of quiet joy and deep gratitude as I drifted into sleep, dreaming of possibilities.

The next day, Bill encouraged me to take it easy after the rigorous pace of the last two weeks. I am a self-confessed bookworm. Should I have a stay-in-bed-and-read-a-book day? No, I took out the eggs, green onions, peppers, mushrooms, and cheese to make an omelette. Today, anything was possible, but there were things that couldn't wait. First and most important, I had to see my kids. I spent most of the day with Kristianne and the boys catching up on the events of the last two weeks. I did most of the talking because my two weeks away had been more eventful than hers, and she was a great listener. Then I went with them for the boys' scheduled appointment with their pediatrician.

My home routine had suffered a minor derailment in my absence. I needed to reclaim my space and, following an old compulsion, I tackled each room aggressively with a ritualistic cleaning, dusting where there was no visible dust and tidying throughout the house. Call it a character flaw, but I simply had to get this done, otherwise it would nag at my head for days to come. Everything clean and in its space, for me, makes life simpler.

I wondered what I should do as I eased into my new normal. Not to sound glib, but the time pressure was now over. Still, I would have been naive to think that back on my home turf, I could simply shrug off the intensity of the last two weeks to find peace in the small commonplace routines of daily life. No, I felt self-imposed pressure to keep my nose to the proverbial grindstone. I thought of this as phase two and believed that this phase would likely be more challenging than anything so far accomplished.

In my resolve to get the job done, I was impatient just when I knew I needed as much patience as I could muster. I had a history of being an impatient perfectionist in my work, more interested in the long-term view than the details of the tasks. You'd think a woman who's lived as long as I have and with my work history would have accumulated a canola field of patience, but it was still a lack in the list of my virtues. I remember as a child having frequent discussions with my father on my need and desire to develop this capacity. I admired him tremendously. He was the epitome of patience, as he needed to be with thirteen children. Every New Year's Day after a sumptuous celebratory brunch prepared by my mother, who could fix the best meals this side of heaven, he would give our family his traditional blessing for the New Year. Then he would give each of us, in turn, his wishes and encouragement for success in the year ahead. Funny thing how the focal point of that brief but important exchange for me often was on the topic of developing patience. Bullseye! I worked on mastering that ever-elusive goal throughout my life, and I knew that the time had come. In my role as Executor, I would be called upon to use all the patience I could muster. In the words of Aristotle, "Patience is bitter, but the fruit is sweet." I hoped this process would bring out the best in me.

The Executor role isn't child's play and, partly because of the emotions involved, it's also not for cowards. It's astonishing how often the word "courage" appears in the Executor literature. I'm not surprised by this finding. In the exercising of my role, I had to summon up courage on a daily basis. Courage to keep learning, for example, and to stay committed when the expectation was that as the Executor, I was expected to know exactly what to do and to get it right, right out of the gate. This is not a process of trial and error, of proceeding in full flight by the seat of your pants. There are many variables to manage, with little room for mistakes. Leaders are perpetual learners, I've been told. Well, I must be a great leader, I reasoned, tongue-in-cheek, because I still had a lot to learn about this multidimensional role. I pulled out my Estate books, stacked them in order of usefulness (having cleared my desktop, which was now dedicated for this purpose only), and carved out time each day to research and read the materials.

I pulled out a book from the stack in front of me, not looking for anything specific but in search of inspiration. I flipped the pages, idly watching the page numbers, the chapter titles, the paragraphs flutter by, and then stuck my fingers in at random, like the best of fortune tellers do. The term "Executor Year" leapt off the page. I had stumbled upon the term in my earlier readings and had flagged the paragraph. This term is used as a rule of thumb, underscoring the expectation that a reasonable period of time for settling an average estate in probate is one year from the date of the Executor receiving the Grant of Probate. The settlement of a complex estate may take several years. Not that I posted a countdown calendar, but the Executor year timeframe became my benchmark, my window within which I would complete a long list of critical tasks.

My intuition was setting off alarm bells, and I worried I would miss a critical step, still mysterious to me, coiled tightly in the background somewhere waiting to spring out and bite me in the ass. I accelerated my readings of the textbooks and Executor documents, methodically researching a section each day, underlining and highlighting important sections, attaching sticky notes as page markers wherever I left marginalia. It's not enough to have many pieces when solving a puzzle. You have to have the right pieces at the right time, and you have to know how to use them. To make sure I did, I reached for the notebook I had left neglected for a couple days and recommenced my daily practice of making notes, setting goals, and keeping track. This time, however, I was struck by how the principles of project management would be a very fitting approach to the life-cycle of the Executor's work in uncovering and untangling the elements of the estate and eventually reaching closure. I now saw the Executor as the project manager responsible for the creative work of crafting the path, a roadmap for success, the logistics from beginning to end, and accountable for the success of the process leading to the required deliverable— full distribution of the assets as directed by the will.

Yes, I was the project manager, My Marilyn Project, a largely solitary pursuit. I had mastered endless projects over time, figuring out the angles, calculating the dollars and cents, the timing of start and finish, the risks and benefits, the needed resources, the detailed steps. Small steps. Big steps. But always one step at a time with carefully crafted business plans and project proposals. I had a knack for seeing the big picture and was known to use flip charts and diagrams and arrows at times to point the way. Everything just takes planning. But between you and me, a little luck goes a long way. Actually, here's where a GPS with the power to generate an executorship road map would be incredibly handy. I structured my notes inspired by the anticipated benefits of the well-known PDSA Cycle. Forgive me for an imperfect process, but at the risk of sounding like an underachiever nerd, I stopped short of developing a Gantt chart.

15

December 1, 2017

—

The Morrisseau Question

Accepting death stoically, if you're the Executor, means moving from your grief to taking care of the operational details of the estate. I know as I say it that it seems harsh, but it's the truth. Executorship forces life to move on. There were no *big* things happening with the estate, just details of various degrees of granularity to look after on an ongoing basis. Some activities occurred sequentially, others in parallel and initiated by other parties over which I had no control. I had jumped with both feet into the weeds, and this was without doubt another time of transition, with delays that seemed heavy with implications and consequences serious enough, at least in my mind, to imperil my emotional equilibrium if I didn't take action.

I had by now decided, if not to embrace and relish uncertainty, to at least stop struggling with it, to graciously accept time delays as well as what I could control and what I couldn't. I attended to the details that either came to me unexpectedly or that I initiated

161

to keep things humming along toward my intended deadline. Things were happening whether I liked it or not. I had to adjust, to learn to work within two extremes, some days feeling a weariness that came from lack of advancement rather than lack of energy. Other days I was steeped in the details. I made decisions. I paid off debts. I made calls. I received and sent emails. I made notes. I wrote letters. I sent off requests. I signed documents and popped them in the mail. Those days were full and challenging, with progress achieved step by visible step through sustained, determined effort and with time taken to ask myself whether I was doing the right thing and doing it right. Settled and unsettled became my new normal and symbolic of how the year unfolded.

Friday, December 1, 2017

I got a call from Capri Insurance informing me they would issue a refund of $23.00 to Marilyn's estate and would return to me the death certificate and the certified will I had sent them with my letter, since they believed I would be needing them again. I appreciated their thoughtfulness.

I also received my first estate mail from the Canada Pension Plan, advising me that they had received the information needed and would be sending me the death benefit. The CPP benefit and Old Age Security are paid to the deceased for the month of death. The CPP Death Benefit is an additional lump-sum payment paid to the estate of the deceased up to a maximum of $2,500. The final amount is calculated based on the person's contributions during a qualifying period and is intended by the plan to help defray the funeral costs. I calculated that Marilyn's estate would be receiving the full $2,500, a substantial amount that would, as intended, help cover the funeral expenses. It's important to know that one has to apply for this benefit. In my case, the notification of death and this application were documents completed by the funeral director for my signature. I found out that it's important to keep track of the arrival of this payment when my friend told me the story of how she called the CPP inquiring about the payment she was expecting six months ago only to find out that they had planned to make the payment but had filed the document because of a postal strike and had forgotten about it. They were very apologetic, and her cheque arrived within two weeks of her call. *Thanks for the heads-up*, I thought. Follow-up is on my list.

Not a day went by that the estate details didn't haunt my consciousness with all the pieces at play and their associated risks and complications. I felt on the clock, a bit like my experience of many years on call 24/7. At home, busy with paperwork or cleaning up the house or preparing a meal, some ticking metronome in my mind keep my attention fixed on Executor developments, on the next tasks on or off my list. I think it's fair to say that this haunting, this obsession to leave no barriers to the flow of progress, is what kept my feet planted firmly on the prescriptive path that spells success in the Executor role. It gave me satisfaction (Why deny it?) to check my notes regularly, wanting to be productive and to make sure I didn't miss anything as I quite thoroughly second guessed myself.

It was all nose in, fingers in on this job. No place for one foot in and one foot out. Determined to not drop the ball, I checked my inbox for a fresh batch of emails first thing every morning. I responded to these on evenings and weekends too, whenever they came, but I otherwise blocked time on odd days for the estate: Mondays, Wednesdays and Fridays, keeping sacred the two days a week I spent with Noah. I found it helpful to create some kind of routine, like pockets of control, a rhythm to my days and weeks. Some days I was adamant that this work was nothing more than a specialized area of business. Other days I felt chosen, walking a privileged path created just for me, a spiritual journey. Working through loss. Stopping and starting project pieces. Cultivating patience in waiting for the work of others, for goodwill, for key decisions from overwhelmed systems, abiding in all decisions with the dictates of the will. These were all components of the Executor's journey, of course. They were also an opportunity to test myself and be at peace with the world.

My life changed during this time in unexpected ways, in ways that might wear away at your psyche if you're an extrovert but that were comfortable with my personality. I became quieter, more introverted than ever, finding the experience that was consuming so much of my time wasn't easy to share with acquaintances, friends, or family other than my children, who were interested in the updates and sympathetic with the challenges. Certainly not a topic for a family gathering or social event. Not dinner party conversation.

I found it challenging to explain the Executor process because while I had stockpiled a lot of information in my head for when I'd need it, I was, paradoxically, still uncovering all the layers myself, learning as I went. Some days I fantasized a kindred spirit, but it was clear that for many, my current work was a topic that created great discomfort. Wills and estates were a taboo subject to be avoided. I was baffled by this initially, accustomed as I was to open conversations about every topic, but I came to accept that this attitude is likely driven by the need to reflect on our inevitable demise if we're to focus our attention on wills and estates. Denial might be more comfortable than thoughts of the underground condo. In addition to the limited understanding of the Executor process, which is understandable for anyone who's not had exposure, there is not much sympathy for the Executor. Some people think of this role as a bad-guy-role. The jargon is complicated, with terms one tends to learn not in conversation but in textbooks. A brief explanation often led to:

"I don't know how you do it. Better you than me."

Or a quick dismissive, "Piece of cake!"

Or "Why are you're doing it? This is a job you pass on to others."

Or "Why is it taking you so much time? When will you be finished?"

Curiously, no one, other than my kids, offered to help, including those who would be the first to support a person obviously deeply into the grieving process.

How I do it is one task at a time and then another, as demonstrated in my journey. The question of why may be more difficult for others, but for me it's simple: I made a promise. This isn't all selfless, because my attitude is that I'm paying-it-forward. One day when tomorrow starts without me, preferably when I'm leaving the world as a wrinkled super-centenarian, I want someone devoted to doing the same for me and my progeny.

Saturday, December 2

How can we get an answer, to the Morrisseau question? I noodled on this again and again with no real inspiration until one morning while I was washing the breakfast dishes. There, with no effort on my part, I was struck with a great idea, seemingly coming out of nowhere and gift-wrapped in the colours of the season. *That's it*, I thought. *I have to tell Ana.*

Email to Ana:

Re: *Morriseau Painting*

"I'm thinking it might be worth a visit to the Bearclaw Gallery in Edmonton. Someone there may be able to help us, since they specialize in First Nations, Metis, and Inuit art. I've been there many times and found wonderful people there. I know it takes precious time. No pressure."

Monday, December 4

I decided to call the Institute of Contemporary Art on Portage Avenue to inquire about the Morrisseau painting. They advised me that they don't do authentications and referred me to the Winnipeg Art Gallery, where they are currently in the process of authenticating a Morrisseau painting in their collection. Of course, they were closed. A Wednesday call ended up on the list in my notebook.

Jason emailed. He's worried. Will he have to pay taxes on his inheritance? The answer is no. The good news is that an inheritance of money and the value of the lovely jewellery he'll be receiving is not considered taxable in Canada. I asked him to let his cousins know, since they were likely to have the same question.

I called Adam and asked him to settle an account for the nursing care provided to Marilyn in her home the week before her death. He wasn't sure he could do that before probate completion. He needed the invoice and a copy of the Representative Agreement. I urged him to do it because I believed it was fair to pay the caregiver for her devoted care without delay. I wanted to close this file and popped the appropriate documents in the mail the same day.

Wednesday, December 6

A return call from the Winnipeg Art Gallery:

"Authentication is not a service the WAG can provide. We suggest you contact the Art Dealers Association of Canada. They provide appraisals and represent the largest group of major private galleries in Canada. Perhaps they will be able to help you. Best of luck."

I was happy to receive an email from Irene confirming, on behalf of the accounting firm, that the death certificate and the will had been sent to Germany.

December 12

Adam emailed to let me know he'd received authorization from his manager to pay for the nursing care as I had requested. He now needed my authorization as Executor to release the funds. I sent my authorization by return email. Time and again I reflected on what a marvellous blessing today's technology is in the process of getting all these details attended to. I sent thanks to the gods that be each time a piece of the puzzle fell into place with a simple click on my keyboard.

The payments were evident in the account summary details I received from the bank at the end of each month. I appreciated this report. It made it easy for me to track the Estate funds.

In the afternoon, I called Interior Tax and File with a question for my accountant. Marilyn had been receiving a pension from Germany, a residual pension benefit her husband, Richard, had earned during his working years there. I'd seen in her files that she'd been paying income taxes to the German Government on this pension each year, and I needed my accountant's advice on how to proceed with this. Well, providence provided, as it always does. It so happened that my accountant, Paul, who is worth his weight in gold in so many ways, was currently in Germany, where his daughter attended school. We made a plan: I would send his office certified copies of the death certificate and the will, which they would forward to him. He would take them to the German CRA equivalent, and the process would unfold from there.

Irene also informed me that I would need to send them the required documents at tax time, including not only Marilyn's income but also the usual applicable medical expenses and charitable donations.

"The process is the same as that used for a living person," she told me. "An estate is considered to be a 'taxpayer in its own right, but the due date for filing the return is determined by the date of death. If the death occurred between January1 and October 31, the tax return is due by April 30 of the following year. For Marilyn, who passed away between November 1 and December 31, the final return will be due six months after the date of her death. Penalties will be applied if the return is filed late. Also, taxes owing must be paid by this time, and interest will be added to the final tax bill if the taxes owing are not paid by this deadline."

I appreciated Irene's help. In my readings, I saw the estate defined as everything the person owns at the time of death. It includes both their property and their debts. Settling the estate involves paying the individual's income tax, like all other debts, before the assets can be distributed to the beneficiaries.

Wednesday, December 13

I received a letter from Fortis B.C. addressed to Marilyn's estate with an invoice and informing me that the next reading would be on or about January 22, 2018. Really! One has to have a sense of humour. In fact, the ability to see the funny side kept me on an even keel throughout the process.

Another email note to Adam. It was incredible and wonderful that I could do all this banking business in Kelowna from my home in Winnipeg. I couldn't have found a more helpful bank anywhere. Thank you for your help.

That day I received a Christmas card in the mail from Marilyn's cousins in Germany. I knew that Michael had called to inform them of Marilyn's passing, but their card must have already been in the mail. I made a point of picking up a sympathy card to send them with a note on the stories Marilyn told about the cousins she had visited with Richard and had grown to love.

Thursday, December 14

Email from Jack

Re: *Aloha*

I hope you're doing well and it isn't too cool there.

Why Marilyn's place isn't rented yet is beyond me, as I know there are a lot of folks in Kelowna looking for a place to live, but you and I can read into that. Yesterday they hung up her blinds and I saw a carpet man leaving a few days ago.

For some people in this world they seem to think the more money they have the better they become. Man, they have a lot to learn.

But I hope that you and your family have a truly beautiful Christmas and nothing but the best to you in the coming year.

Germaine, it's been an honour to have met you and to have the pleasure of your company over a drink, so until next time—Aloha.

The news that the apartment was not yet rented out was very disappointing after all the effort we'd put into vacating it on time; however, nothing we could do about it.

Saturday, December 16

Email from Ana:

Re: *Morrisseau Painting*

I picked up the mementos from Marilyn in Kelowna. Thank you for packaging these for me.

*Perhaps some good news on the Morrisseau. Your idea to
go to the Bearclaw Gallery in Edmonton was a great one. I
asked the clerk there this afternoon if anyone in the gallery
was knowledgeable about Morrisseau's work, and we were
directed to a woman by the name of Maria Bailey. She was
absolutely lovely and very helpful. I gave her the background
info on the painting. When I showed her the photo, she was
of the opinion that it might be an original, painted perhaps in
the late 60s or early 70s. And she thinks the painting is beautiful. She also thinks the frame looks like an original. I told her
the painting is currently in Kelowna. Her recommendations:*

*Contact Phil at the Hambleton Gallery in Kelowna. We can
ask Phil to look at the painting and say we were referred
by Maria.*

*Or she would be willing to view the painting at the Bearclaw
Gallery if we want to bring it there.*

*With respect to where to sell the painting if it's an original,
she said most galleries take a 40% commission on the sale
price. Paintings can be sold at auctions if we choose to go that
route. Walkers Fine Art and Estate Auction in Toronto is highly
recommended. She said Walkers recently sold a Morrisseau
about the same size as this one for $70,000.*

*Probably not a good idea right now to get too excited about
its potential value. Call me when you have time so we can
discuss this in more detail.*

She then called Phil and sent him the photo.

His response: "It is an interesting image, but I cannot say
exactly what value it would have until I see it in the flesh. It is certainly of an earlier style and the cloth it is painted on is unusual. I

will reserve further comment until I see it. I will look at it for you if you bring it in the first week of January."

Wednesday, December 20, 2018

I emailed David Wright asking for an update on the probate process and sending him financial details to add to the list of assets and liabilities.

Wednesday, January 4, 2018

Email from Julia

> Re: *Norval Picture*
>
> *I just came from the Hambleton Gallery. Unfortunately, they believe we have a silk screen that is of no significant value. She showed me an original they have in the gallery and there is definitely a difference. So that's a bummer but we're not too disappointed. Michael says his mother told him years ago that it was not valuable.*

Michael's story unfolded. His understanding was that Marilyn acquired this painting from a physician who lived in her condo building. She liked a painting that Marilyn owned, so they traded. But Marilyn never displayed it in her home.

My response to Julia:

> Re: *Norval Picture*
>
> *I was really hoping it was an original worth at least $70,000. It is an interesting piece, and someone will want it for sure if the kids decide to sell it. Well, we now know, and we can put this piece of the estate to rest.*

It was a worthwhile pursuit, I thought. We learned a number of interesting things about the art world, and it was quite fun playing detective.

Tuesday, January 2, 2018

A cheque arrived in the mail from Medical Services Plan of British Columbia with a letter advising me that coverage had now been cancelled and this was a refund on the balance in her account.

Monday, January 22, 2018

The death benefit arrived in today's mail. It took only two months to process the benefit. Not bad, I thought for a government agency. I put the cheque back in the mail on its way to Adam for deposit in the estate account.

16

January 22, 2018

—

Relationships

It's impossible to spend a day doing business without appreciating the wonders of our current technology and how it impacts on every aspect of our lives. Today, however, I was reflecting on the one thing that remains the same—the mystery of human interaction—the relationship with the beneficiaries that simply can't be addressed with a keyboard click. With such a large stake in the outcome, what would be important to them? What would they want to know? What would they care about? Were they worried about things? What were they thinking about the process so far? What would I need to do to keep us all on the same page?

The integrity of our relationship would really boil down to four factors:

1. Mutual trust and respect.

2. The beneficiaries' understanding the importance of the will as the driver of all my decisions as Executor.

3. The beneficiaries knowing that my commitment was to work on their behalf to maximize their legacy.

4. Strong ongoing communication to generate a sense of safety and confidence in the process.

I was mindful that regular communication with the beneficiaries would be one of the most important Executor strategies during this entire process of estate management. Adequate communication would take time and effort, but, in my view, that would be the most enjoyable part of the work. Human connection during the process of settling an estate is critical, as it is in any other work of importance. The relationship isn't a one-way street, but the Executor has to take the initiative. The literature emphasizes that frequent and effective communication with the beneficiaries is essential to success in building and maintaining rapport and avoiding uncomfortable conversations or confrontations. Beneficiaries, like anyone else involved in an important relationship, don't want to be kept in the dark. This wasn't a new concept for me, given my years of work in professional environments where good communication is of paramount importance.

The Executor doesn't need to be an extrovert with extraordinary people skills but must embrace the fact that beneficiaries need to understand what's going on and be prepared to provide information, to listen and answer their questions. Beneficiaries will hate long periods of silence while the Executor is busy working on their behalf. They, unlike the Executor, are not immersed in the management of the estate and have no idea of the process's steps, so there's a need to explain, simplify, and demystify what they may perceive as a complex process. They don't want to be surprised, the literature highlights.

Failure to communicate, it seems, is the number one complaint against Executors. Beneficiaries need to know the Executor's agenda. No news will be perceived as bad news. If they don't hear from the Executor, beneficiaries might think something fishy is going on and start checking up on the Executor, looking over her shoulder by phone or text or email. They won't know if the Executor has a lot of fires on her plate to deal with and that she's not trying to keep them in the dark on purpose.

I was committed to being proactive with regular status reports and clear updates intended to inform and avoid misunderstanding, sadness, and drama, keeping in mind the need for extra effort given the distance and lack of opportunity for in-person interactions. Whether face-to-face or by email or text message, the interface is person to person, not person to Siri. The trouble with email or text is that although it generally works well for communicating facts, it leaves a lot of room for misinterpretation, and it's not so great for building an emotional connection, a relationship that touches beyond the surface. A clear advantage for us was that we already had a strong long-term emotional connection.

There's plenty of research that shows that people prefer to do business with someone they feel comfortable with on a personal level. Executorship is business. One thing rings true in this as in other areas of business life: beneficiaries come with all kinds of personalities, including those who don't play well with others. We're all emotional beings, and family tensions can escalate in these personal processes. Sometimes people's worst colours jump out when money and personal possessions associated with their heritage are involved. Individual moods and temperament all affect the quality of the interaction, and the Executor must respond accordingly, at times drawing on improvisational skills to sustain collaboration.

Fortunately in this case, we were at ease with each other. There was magic in our relationship. Marilyn's beneficiaries were not nameless people but individuals I cared about. I was convinced that they knew I had their best interests at heart, and I wanted them to understand the complexities and challenges of the process, not only the achievements. I would speak simply and honestly, distilling the work into clear next steps, even when the truth might be messy at times. I would want them to also know when I needed their support. This approach, I believed, would sustain our relationship of trust and loyalty. Also, this opportunity for learning was congruent with my commitment to Michael as we began the journey together at Marilyn's bedside. I made a practice of copying Julia and Michael in all my correspondence with the three beneficiaries. Whereas Michael had been my right hand in the work on site in Kelowna, Julia had become my active connection with the beneficiaries, my email partner. This was clearly her medium. She was the person who responded when no one else did, who asked questions and made things happen. She was of tremendous help on my journey—an act of generosity I won't forget.

My email to the beneficiaries:

January 22, 2018

Re: *Marilyn's Estate—Cash/Coin Box Inventory*

After procrastinating for a while, I have finally completed the inventory of the cash box Marilyn kept in her dresser drawer. You'll see the listing on the attached document. I met with my bank advisor for advice on how to proceed with these contents. He told me that banks will only take paper money and that they provide only the face value of the cash. So, for example, if an old one dollar bill is now worth $1.20, they will only give you one dollar for it.

The coins would have to be dealt with through a coin dealer, or, for example, the American coins would have to be exchanged for Canadian money somewhere before the bank would take them.

So the option is for me to cash these coins—don't know how I would do it at this point, but I know that it would take time and effort.

The cash and coins are not in m̄int condition. They have all been in circulation, which detracts from their value. I've searched the internet and found their incremental value to be insignificant. They may be worth more down the road. And since you're young, you might have an interest in holding on to them.

Please discuss among the three of you and let me know what you'd like done with these. If you decide to keep them, I will bring the box with me on my next visit.

Thanks a bunch. I will look forward to hearing from you.

January 30, 2018

Email from Julia

Re: *Coins*

Have you heard back from any of the kids about this? I told my kids to talk it over with Jason and get back to you. Let me know and I will get them moving on it.

My response:

Hi, Julia. No, I have not yet heard from the three muske-teers. Good if you can give them a prompt. I'd like to know their decision.

17

—

Grant of Probate

I received from David the Affidavit of Assets and Liabilities sent in the mail. He advised me that with the affidavit now complete, and with my approval, he would proceed with filing the probate documents with the Kelowna Court Registry, anticipating an eight to ten week timeframe for the court to grant probate. I gave him the OK to proceed.

I received a refund cheque in the mail from Shaw Cable and sent it to Adam for the account. He was always there to help, and I thanked him every time I sent him correspondence of any kind, actually every chance I got. Giving thanks can feel beautiful.

Friday, February 2, 2018

David sent an email confirming the notices to family had been sent. He noted that these notices are not meant to solicit a response necessarily but only to give the recipient notice that I am applying for probate. In closing, his note affirmed that this part of the estate work was going smoothly but slowly and reminded me that these processes take time. I wasn't surprised but pleased to see that David's formal correspondence began with condolences extended to the family members.

Saturday, March 3, 2018

Email to Irene

> Re: *Estate taxes*

> *I've placed all the information for the preparation of Marilyn's tax return in today's mail so they should get to you next week. Thank you so much for all your help.*

In response, she sent me a Client Data Sheet to complete for Marilyn's 2017 tax year and return to her. This is a standard form that would allow her firm access to the information needed for tax filing.

Saturday, March 31, 2018

Email to the beneficiaries:

Re: *Happy Easter*

> *Hello, everyone. Happy Easter—may the Easter Bunny find his way to your homes bringing beautiful sunshine and all the abundance of spring.*

> *Just FYI, we are still awaiting probate. I'm sure you're thinking it's taking a long time for these legal processes; however, our lawyer says this is normal. I will be in touch with you as soon as I hear confirmation.*

Thursday, April 5, 2018

I was on a break, binging on *Gilmore Girls*, when Zachary arrived for a short play time.

"Guess what, Zachary, today is my oldest sister, Tante Lucie's, birthday. She is 80 years old. Can you believe that? Eighty candles on her birthday cake. That's pretty close to 100."

"Well, guess what, Grammia, my wolverine mama is 79 years old. And she runs really fast."

We have to have some fun in the mix.

Friday, April 13, 2018

Email from David

> Re: *Grant of Probate*

> *We have received notice today that the Grant of Probate has been issued and is ready for pickup at the Kelowna Law Courts upon payment of probate fees. You may either arrange for payment of these fees by our office "in trust" or we can pay them on behalf of the estate and collet them back once we render our accounts, which will be sometime next week. Let us know whether you'd like to pay us these funds in trust or have us pay them on behalf of the estate. We'll be fine either way.*

My return email:

> *Thank you for your work on this task, David. It would be great if you would pay the fees on behalf of the estate.*

I now have a fixed date for the Executor year: April 13, 2019. Seems like a lot of time to achieve my goal. I think to myself, *What a wonderful world. We have the Grant of Probate. Yeah! We have just turned a sharp corner. We're on a roll!*

Monday, April 16, 2018

Email from David:

> Re: *Grant of Probate*
>
> *As discussed, we have now retrieved the Grant of Probate and have attached a scanned copy for your records.*

Wednesday, April 18

Email received from David confirming that he had not received any word of dispute or disagreement in response to his correspondence with the family.

We talked on the telephone and considered the option of depositing all funds with the legal firm "in trust." This way, the funds would be readily available to be distributed by his office, upon my instructions, for payment of bills and taxes, with the balance eventually distributed to the beneficiaries. I opted for keeping the funds with Interior Savings, since my work with them had gone so smoothly and I didn't want to relinquish control of the estate assets. This decision had the effect of discontinuing legal services for the remainder of my Executor work. David expressed some surprise, but he understood that I was eager to minimize all expenditures in an effort to retain as much of the estate funds as possible for the beneficiaries. He commented that life is stressful and most people choose to outsource the headaches associated with all the details of estate management. "They simply cannot be bothered," he said. And this was really the foundation for his surprise at my decision. I got where he was coming from, but this decision to do the work myself felt like a prompt from my conscience to do the right thing. I probably didn't know enough about the process yet to fully appreciate his words. Of course, our relationship was such that he would be available should I need his advice going forward—a win-win situation, in my view.

Before we ended our telephone call, he emphasized that I must not distribute the assets to the beneficiaries until six months after receipt of the Grant of Probate. I expressed my surprise and he explained that in British Columbia, children and spouses have up to six months following the issuance of the Grant of Probate to challenge a will. If the Executor distributes the assets before the six month period expires, they can be held personally responsible for any claim made by a family member. If I really wanted to make a distribution prior to the expiration of the six-month period, a lawyer would have the beneficiaries sign a document whereby they give consent to the early distribution of the assets. This way, they wouldn't come back on me later.

Great advice, and I appreciated it. I expressed my heartfelt thanks for his help as we said our goodbye. I really trusted David and enjoyed working with him.

Wednesday, April 25, 2018

Email to beneficiaries

> Re: *Update on Marilyn's Estate*
>
> *I hope you're basking in the spring sunshine. We're finally getting warm days here, and the snow is disappearing. I will be gardening soon.*
>
> *I'm happy to tell you that we have now received the Grant of Probate for Marilyn's Estate, dated April 13, 2018. The law in B.C. requires a waiting period of six months after probate for the distribution of assets. This takes us to October 13 before I can proceed with the distribution. That's Ok, because it will take about that long before the tax process is complete*

and I receive clearance from the CRA. I will look forward to seeing you in the fall and will be in touch with specifics as the months go by.

Thursday, April 26, 2018

Return Email from Julia:

Thanks for the update. I'm hoping to get out to do some gardening work too. All's well here. The kids just finished writing final exams. We will look forward to seeing you in the fall then.

Monday, April 30, 2018

Canada Post brought me a fat envelope from David's office. His letter confirmed the information we'd shared on the telephone. It also emphasized several of my responsibilities as Executor—things I already knew, but I appreciated his conscientious reminder. His letter was very thorough, and I realized that in doing this he was placing the responsibility squarely on my shoulders and off his now that he was no longer acting on my behalf. His letter:

1. Advised me to open a bank account in the name of the estate.

2. Outlined my responsibility as Executor to file the appropriate Income Tax Returns on behalf of the deceased and the estate, which reminded me of the saying that the only certainties in life are death and taxes. It cautioned me that if I failed to do so, I may be personally responsible for payment of any tax owing.

3. Advised me to make sure to obtain a Clearance Certificate from the CRA. This is an official document

certifying that all taxes, interest, or penalties under the Income Tax Act and chargeable under the assets of the estate have been paid.

4. Provided contact information for the Canada Pension Office should I need to contact their office regarding Canada Pension benefits.

5. Confirmed that I would attend to the transmission of the assets to the beneficiaries according to the will and emphasized that I must not do so before the expiration of 210 days from the date of the issuance of the Grant of Probate unless I obtained consent for an earlier distribution from all beneficiaries or a court order to do so. It explained that these provisions serve to protect me from liability.

6. Recommended that I obtain a Release from the beneficiaries before distributing the assets.

7. Enclosed two copies of the Grant of Probate, copies of the probate application documents filed in the Kelowna Court Registry, and all documents from his file for my records. These included a copy of all the documents I signed in his office before leaving Kelowna.

8. Included his statement of account for services rendered and for disbursements incurred. I was actually shocked at how minimal the legal expenses were. The probate fees were included, as expected, as part of his disbursements.

9. Finished with thanks and an invitation to contact him should I have any questions or need for further services.

This letter prompted a question I didn't have the answer to: How long would I be expected to keep estate documents after distribution of assets is complete and the estate is closed? I had to research the question and found that important estate documents such as trusts, wills, birth and death certificates, Social Security information, and marriage and divorce certificates should all be kept indefinitely. I also discovered that the CRA doesn't make a distinction for the records of deceased taxpayers. These records should be kept by the Executor of the person's estate, including the receipts used to calculate reductions, for a solid seven years. The advice is to keep copies of receipts, insurance statements, credit card statements, and bank statements for up to three years. In short, the prudent Executor might as well place the mountain of documents gathered through the process of settling the estate in the bottom drawer of a filing cabinet, close the drawer, and expect to leave it all there for a very long time.

I sent a copy of the Grant of Probate and David's statement of account to Adam, asking him to pay the invoice from the estate account as appropriate, now that we had achieved probate. Adam, always efficient, followed through without delay.

I also received an email from Irene with a copy of Marilyn's tax return, for which she needed my signature. I signed it immediately and sent it back. Her firm would e-file on my behalf.

Thursday, May 24, 2018

The mail kept bringing in bills of one kind or another. On this day I received a statement of account from Interior Health covering Marilyn's accommodations during her stay at Central Hospice. I was expecting this, and the only surprise was how long it took for them to send it to me. I scanned the invoice and emailed it to Adam for payment.

Wednesday, July 25, 2018

I received the Notice of Assessment from the CRA for the 2017 tax year, happy to see a small credit. I had no issues with the Notice of Assessment, so I now had all the information I needed to apply for a Clearance Certificate, a document that provides written confirmation by the CRA that all tax liabilities of the deceased have been paid not only for the year of death but for all prior years as well. The literature emphasizes that if the Executor distributes the assets prior to receiving this Clearance Certificate, the Executor will be held liable for any taxes owing if not enough money is left in the estate to cover the required payment. That Clearance Certificate is a document of utmost importance, since it provides the assurance I need as the Executor confirming that I am relieved of any personal liability for future taxes. I wanted this document in my hands. I downloaded the form "Asking for a Clearance Certificate," feeling pretty proud of myself for finding it. I filled in the blanks and popped it in the mail to the CRA. This was the last piece I needed and now felt confident that all of Marilyn's outstanding debts had been paid.

Friday, August 24, 2018

Email to beneficiaries

Re: *Update on Marilyn's Estate:*

Hello everyone. Just to let you know I have not forgotten you. I am still planning to come in November to finalize the distribution of Marilyn's assets. I will be in touch with you closer to that time when I'm planning the travel details. I hope you're having a good summer despite the hardships of the smoke from forest fires across B.C. I was in Calgary last week where the smoke was so thick, we were forced to stay indoors all week. Air quality conditions were even worse in Edmonton. I hope we all get rain soon.

18

November 4, 2018

—

Executor Release and Indemnity

Sunday, November 4, 2018

It was Daylight Savings Time, a free pass to spend an extra hour of sleep as we peeled our clocks back an hour. I appreciated the extra sleep maybe preparing for the long winter ahead.

Wednesday, November 14, 2018

I sent an email to Adam confirming my trip to Kelowna December 3 to 5 and setting a meeting time for 2:30 December 3.

Monday, November 19, 2018

Email to beneficiaries

> Re: *Important Communication*

> *My condolences, once again, on this important anniversary. I miss my friend Marilyn, as I'm sure you do.*

As I'm preparing to complete the administration of Marilyn's estate, I'm sending you the following documents for your review:

1. The Statement of Assets and Liabilities prepared by David Wright showing the value of Marilyn's estate at the time of her death.

2. The Executor's Statement of Receipts and Disbursements showing the current balance in the chequing and savings account, the Registered Income Fund Account, and the members' shares account, all now consolidated in the estate account.

3. A note on the contents of the safety deposit box, and

4. A statement of unpaid Executor expenses. Please note that I have not charged any fees for my work in the role of Executor.

If you have any questions about these documents, please don't hesitate to ask. Call me or email. I will be happy to hear from you.

I will be in Kelowna from Monday, December 3 to Wednesday, December 5. I would like to meet with you, Mia, and Trevor on Monday, December 3 or Tuesday, December 4. Please let me know what time would work best for you in the late afternoon or early evening. Jason, it would be great if you could be in Kelowna at that time and available to join us.

I will be distributing the balance of Marilyn's assets at this meeting, in equal shares to each of you with the exception of the designated jewellery. Jason, I will send your share via

*registered mail if you're not available for this meeting. Please
let me know.*

*It's necessary for me to obtain your agreement with the
accounting I've sent you on the disbursements I've incurred in
the administration of the estate. I will need a note from you in
response to this email, indicating that you are satisfied with
the management of the estate and releasing me from further
responsibilities in the role of Executor following distribution of
the remaining assets in early December. Please date and sign
the attached Executor Release and Indemnity document, scan
it, and return it to me as soon as possible.*

*I look forward to hearing from you and very much look
forward to our visit in Kelowna.*

Emailing back and forth, we set a time for Monday, choosing early evening because Jason would be flying in that day from Grande Prairie. Julia invited us for dinner at her home.

I didn't share this with the beneficiaries, but I did tell Julia that I was feeling a little nervous with this plan, because I hadn't yet received the Clearance Certificate from the CRA. "They never call; they never write," I told her, tongue in cheek. I had decided I was willing to take the chance, however, with sufficient confidence after examined in detail seven years' worth of her tax returns in my possession.

The format I used for the Executor Statement of Receipts and Disbursements was a simple document, clear and easy to follow with a column each for the date, the item received, the item paid, and some brief details. There was no demand in this communication for a sophisticated presentation with complicated bells and whistles, and no need for an accountant's complex spreadsheet. A simple chart with detailed, accurate content did the job, a chart that was filled in for the beneficiaries with a detailed account of all the assets and the expenditures in the process and the balance to date, for distribution.

I didn't include a fee for my contributions. One of the biggest drawbacks to serving as Executor is the tremendous amount of time it takes to handle all the responsibilities. While I was very diligent at keeping financial accounts, I made no efforts whatsoever to keep track of my time spent on the work, since I had no intention right from the get-go to line my pockets with a fee for my role. I was able to fit in the work in the flexibility of my retirement lifestyle. My time in this case didn't cost anything, and I wasn't concerned about opportunity cost. While I believe my work provides value and I should be well compensated for it, I've always felt that when I do something for family, it would be done freely. I was happy to donate my services. No debt incurred.

I was aware that Executors may receive an Executor fee up to a specific amount governed by provincial legislation. This amount, another factor for the Executor to know, is one that varies significantly across provinces. In British Columbia, the Executor is entitled, under the Trustees Act, to a compensation of 5% of the value of the estate. This fee is to cover the Executor's time, pains, trouble, and labour, and is allowable unless the Executor compensation has been otherwise specified in the will. Marilyn's will was silent on this matter. No doubt I've had my share of trouble, pains, and labour, but I believe Marilyn knew I would take this on not for status or power or income but as a service added to my list of the manifold expressions of love for her and her family, as well as my determination to maximize her legacy for her grandchildren. Compensation received as an Executor fee, by the way, is considered to be taxable income.

The Executor Release and Indemnity form I sent the beneficiaries for their signature and immediate return to me is a document intended to confirm that the beneficiaries are satisfied with the expenditures shown in the accounts and with my handling of the estate. It also gives me assurance that they won't change their minds on this and complain in the future. The signed document protects me from personal liability for future claims against the estate. Not that I expected the beneficiaries to be dissatisfied. Common sense told me right from the start to tread carefully with all expenditures. Executorship is not a time to play fast and loose with someone else's money. Every expenditure was carefully considered, and I knew that was reflected in the precision of the documents I so meticulously kept. I had become a documentarian of every step, certain this attention to detail would pay off. I would have been ready to submit these useful metrics, if asked, at any time. Submitting them to the beneficiaries at this stage was essential—I needed their approval before I could proceed with the next steps. Expenditures from here on in would be limited to a predictable few, such as the accounting fees.

I was very pleased at their return of the signed Executor Release and Indemnity document the very next day, all three of them sending thanks for my work on their behalf. A wise woman doesn't need thanks, I've often thought, just results, but maybe my emotional reserves were a little tapped out, since their gratitude hit the mark and meant a lot to me. It felt good to have my work and care appreciated. I have heard many times in my career that business is business, it isn't personal. Hogwash to that, I say. This executorship business is personal to me, because I care deeply about completing my mission in the best possible way and with the greatest expediency. I want my personal devotion to the task to result in a great experience for the three beneficiaries. That is exactly what Marilyn wanted from me. My focus, discipline, pacing, and meticulous organization were paying off, I assured her: "We're getting there now, and attention to the remaining details is key to last the distance. I will work like a Trojan to see it through."

Business is sometimes a funny thing, I thought as an aside. I was recently preparing my four-year-old Noah for an experience with his mother in her work environment where she would introduce him to her colleagues. I decided it would be important for him to know the basics, so I coached him in doing the proper handshake expected in a business setting. Stand tall. Look the person in the eyes. Give them a nice, warm smile. Extend your arm. Make sure your grasp is firm, not soft like a marshmallow, and say, "How do you do?"

We practised a few times and then his mom came home from work and it was time for a demo. She had been warned: "Be ready for a big moment." I'm proud to tell you he did a stellar job, a virtuoso of confidence—great posture, unwavering eye contact, and a lovely smile at his mother. She extended her hand, looking into the face of her pure mischief-maker, and said, "How do you do?" With the practiced ease of a trickster, he held out a steady hand for a firm grip. Then with all the warmth and sincerity of a life insurance salesman one month away from his monthly quota, he said, "How do you *poo*?" Then he ran away hooting with wild laughter. A friend once told me, "If you want to improve your life, learn to laugh often and to laugh out loud." I agree with her and think what a powerful thing laughter is. In the midst of a demanding process, a moment for laughter is sometimes just as helpful as words of thanks.

Thursday, November 22, 2018

The CRA Clearance Certificate arrived in the mail. Yeah! I would be lying if I didn't admit that right up to that moment I'd worried about that loose end. The timing was fantastic! It gave me a buzz of happiness to think we would indeed get everything done on December 3.

Wednesday, November 28, 2018

An Executor knows the value of timing, and my real life didn't stop when I was not immersed in estate management. The rhythm of the year provided built-in breaks from the work and served to keep me healthy and productive. Once away from the work, even if only for a bit of time, I forgot about it completely. This is what I told myself as Bill and I boarded a flight to Calgary for an early Christmas gathering at the home of our beloved Anthony, Karmon, and Elise before going on to conclude the estate business in Kelowna. I hadn't seen my children in too long a while and couldn't wait to get there. We would have Christmas this weekend and again on December 25. The exceptional benefit of celebrating Christmas twice is a phenomenon I was sure must bring good luck. Christmas is the time of year I cherish most, but here's the funny thing: I think of Christmas as a state of mind, with its essence untouched by time or place. I make no attempt to recreate the Christmas of my childhood and would be equally happy with a Christmas in July if it meant time with my kids.

We were greeted with loving enthusiasm. Elise, who was so excited, started bounding down the stairs when she heard the garage door open. She immediately guided us with great pride to the elegant Christmas tree in their living room. She's a good girl prepared for Santa's coming and completely delighted with the magic of the season.

Today's values of splash and bigness tend to devalue the grandmother spending her day playing with her grandchild. Not in my world. I'm reminded in my time with her to delight in the small things, to choose happiness.

We colour together on the same page, a perfect tête-a-tête. We cut and glue and create and build and make marble runs and play scrabble and read books. And then she's full of jumping beans and

I laugh and applaud her cartwheels, handstands, and prowess with the hula hoop.

This is for me the perfect fairy tale with nothing else I want to be doing during those days in which she is the centre of my world. I hold those moments of profound peace and happiness close to my chest like a miser, tremendously jealous of my treasure.

Friday, November 30, 2018

Email to Jack

Re: *Hello*

Hello, Jack. I'm coming to Kelowna December 3 and would love to see you. Do you have time for a cuppa?

Email from Jack.

So cool. I was just thinking of you, and yes I would be honoured. Energy never runs out. Just give me a heads up.

19

—

A New Condition Matters

All too soon, it's time to board our flight to Kelowna. Bill doesn't travel much. He's a recluse by nature, ever since his early childhood. Working in his garage, well stocked with equipment for any project, has more appeal to him than the mysteries of foreign lands or the glamour of all-inclusive resorts and fabulous cruises. The practical consequences of his disability have added a whole new layer of complexity to every journey. Still, to my surprise and delight, he accompanied me to Kelowna for the final disposition of Marilyn's assets. We landed mid-morning, had a long, relaxed brunch, registered at the hotel, unpacked, and went on our way for the meeting with Adam.

We began with the simplest matter—the safety deposit box. We went with Adam to retrieve it and then to reconcile the contents with my original list. Then the closing of the bank account discussion and the moment of surprise—a new condition surfaced that would generate a need to adjust my plan. As Adam leaned forward across the desk, he said, "There's something you should know."

I went on alert at the change in his tone, the sound of warning bells I couldn't ignore, sending a frisson of premonition down my spine.

After an uncomfortable, pregnant pause, he said, "Are you aware that the Registered Income Plan (RIF) becomes considered as income when it's cashed in?"

His words chilled my blood. Why did I feel there was a point floating up there above my head like a kite in a summer breeze? I wondered if it was a bear-trap question. No. Adam had been a huge help. He was on my team. I trusted his intentions.

I stared at him as I sagged in my chair, I'm sure with a look of stunned surprise taking possession of my face as comprehension flooded in. It took a lot of willpower to keep my jaw from dropping.

"What does that mean?" I asked once I found my voice again, afraid to hear the answer and in a tone not of accusation but of barefaced perplexity. I really wanted to say, "You have got to be kidding me" with great emphasis. I refrained, recognizing the expression as unbecoming.

"It means there will be taxes owing on it."

"Wait a second. You're saying I'm going to have to file taxes for 2018?"

"Yes, the estate will need to pay the taxes owing on this amount."

I shook my head in disbelief at this shattering discovery, experiencing a full what-the-hell-do-I-do-now moment. I desperately wanted to be Zachary the shape shifter known to be a shark one moment, a fox or snake the next. I wanted to find a way to step out of my winter boots, open the window, and dive or slither into another life. Anyone's life.

"Now what do I do?" I asked, struggling to find a single coherent thought. I felt like a deflated balloon schooling my voice to calmness as my brain worked on grinding out a solution to this problem. "As you know, Adam, my goal has been to distribute all the assets today. I've set up a meeting with the beneficiaries this evening for this purpose."

Who was it who said "If you want to make God laugh, tell him your plans"? I'm sure he was doubled-over in a good belly laugh right now.

Adam remained calm. "My suggestion would be to keep enough in the account to cover the taxes and to distribute the balance this evening."

I nodded my head in agreement. There wasn't much to think through, really. It was clear I'd hit a wall, and what do you do when you hit a wall? You must push it out of the way by creating the best solution. We didn't have the luxury of indecision.

"This seems to be the only reasonable course of action."

Bill sat in silence beside me, nodding his head in agreement. It was clear we were all thinking the same thing. We decided on an amount and then I asked Adam to prepare a cheque on the balance for each of the beneficiaries. He wanted more time, but I insisted.

"We need this now, given that one of the beneficiaries is flying in, as we speak, from Grand Prairie for this very purpose." Adam consulted his supervisor and they agreed to do it. Bill and I waited while the cheques were being processed and, once again, I felt grateful to Adam for his ongoing efforts to be helpful.

I was still reacting as we waited. Why hadn't I been told that earlier? Had they been speaking in code? Had I missed the memo? Isn't the bank supposed to be a key resource? Isn't making sure clients appreciate the details of complex investment vehicles the role of the banker? The RIF was also included on the list of assets prepared with my lawyer. It really should have been cashed and not shown as a RIF on that document submitted to the court. Why didn't that happen? Did we all have the same blind spot? Who knows? My head was buzzing with these questions as we got in the car, and my reaction was painful. In my red-zone defensiveness, I really wanted to blame someone, but my inner critic showed up in full force: *Time to check your ego at the door. While this is a horribly jagged pill to swallow, you have only yourself to blame. Why didn't you look it up?* In my not-so-blessed ignorance, I had never thought of it. I should have made the connection, since I own a RIF myself, but I hadn't been exposed to the rules of it in this context.

I had learned that there are a number of things to know about investments when managing an estate. The financials as a whole in this context were a bit of a mystery. I had always loved the slow, meticulous solving of such mysteries, but at the moment I wasn't enjoying this one, and I was feeling a twinge of regret at having taken on this role. I would like to claim that my intuition had led me to search the specifics of RIFs in the literature, but that wasn't the case. I didn't wish to be melodramatic, but I couldn't hide in denial or shirk my culpability.

I think of Noah as I write these words. I had him happily playing in the bathtub one day when he was three. At one point he noticed that I saw him holding his penis. Before I had a chance to say a word, he looked at me and said: "Don't worry, Grammia, I peed in my hand. I didn't pee in the bathtub."

Well, I might have held all the right pieces in hand with the very best of intentions but, let's face it, I peed in the tub and it did seem appropriate to blame myself. The truth is, in the Executor role you have to ferret out the details yourself, even if you have a lawyer and an accountant and a banker as advisors. The Executor cannot afford to be complacent. I hadn't purposely put this on the backburner, and maybe off the stove altogether for some time now, but I was the one who dropped the ball. I couldn't go into hiding. I was certainly not willfully blind. I acknowledged the truth that research is a guide only, not a guarantee. Our minds allow us to see only what we have the knowledge to see, and our assumptions can keep us blind. With a single misstep, things can go off the rails very quickly. David and I had begun that financial conversation, but it wasn't enough. I could have cracked the books open at the financial pages a bit more. I had found myself distracted, struggling to concentrate when reading about these financial vehicles, other thoughts at the back of my mind pushing forward for recognition. I would find myself feeling as if I'd dropped down in the middle of a financial textbook, reading and retaining nothing, forced to begin again. If only, I was thinking now, there had been an interesting story, perhaps case histories, built around this information, it would have helped tremendously in sustaining my attention.

Executorship lesson learned: Be diligent in questioning everything you're not sure of. Make sure to ask the dumb questions, because they may not be as banal as they may seem at first blush. Raise your hand if there's been a time in your life when you've been too embarrassed to ask the question on the tip of your tongue. Well, executorship is not a time to worry about appearing unsophisticated. Good advice is just advice, but I don't want to downplay this. Asking questions about how each investment works upon the person's death is of paramount importance in getting the needed answers. In other words, if you don't know your stuff because you haven't asked the right questions, you'll stumble on the tripwires set to catch unaware Executors. Prepare for pain. Only diligence and attention to detail can save you.

Some investments, as I knew from my initial discussion with David and from my readings, are exempt from the probate process. TFSAs fall into that category. The details were all there, a clear picture, in the books on my desk. Now that I knew what to look for, I found other vehicles that qualify to bypass probate. Life insurance is one of them, and I found myself searching Marilyn's financials once again to make sure I didn't miss an insurance policy. I hadn't. I found a lot of interesting information on life insurance in my readings, emphasizing its importance in estate planning. Should you have life insurance? If yes, how much is enough? There are even formulas for calculating one's life insurance needs. What type should you get? How should you choose your agent and insurance company? I wished I'd had that information at my fingertips when I was a youth, and I now wanted my kids to read all this stuff. In the meantime, I discovered that if Marilyn had a life insurance policy, I would simply fill out a claim form and provide the company with the death certificate, and the insurance amount would be sent directly to the beneficiaries, bypassing probate. Good to know.

Of course, I still didn't have full knowledge of all the complicated financial vehicles one can encounter as Executor, but I now had all the information I needed for this estate. I had a solid grip on the financials, a matter that ranked high on my scale of things to know.

I had been sure of myself flying in from Calgary that morning. I had played an imagination game during the flight: I held a picture in my mind of closing the account at the bank and seeing the joyful faces of the beneficiaries as I handed out the funds. Then I saw us raising glasses in celebration of estate closure and finishing the evening with thanks and hugs. The game was instructive as it outlined the ideal process and the happy results.

I had felt confident still an hour ago walking to the security deposit box and checking off the jewels with my original list. Now I felt deflated, like the savoury soufflé of my Thanksgiving brunch after the first serving, the bubble of my enthusiasm and confidence collapsed.

How much does this oversight matter? It won't likely matter to the beneficiaries, who will probably see beyond it. Not to my network of family and friends, who know me to be thorough and whose confidence in me would be hard to shake, even if they knew of this detail. But to myself, the one who clamoured for perfection, the one for whom less than stellar results are seldom acceptable?

Maybe I deserved this dose of humiliation for not having completed my homework thoroughly enough, leaving me floundering in the dark. If only I could call a mulligan and start over so this misstep could be eliminated. The fact is, there is no potential for a mulligan in Estate management. I didn't feel stupid...I felt inept, fully the imposter now having faked executorship for several months.

Perhaps most painful was the thought of having my ignorance exposed in the meeting with the beneficiaries when I'd worked so hard to present as smart and knowledgeable in the world of executorship. The secret would be out. I would feel mortified in the heat of exposure. Would I come across as a dumb ass, way over my head and sinking fast? The Executor cartoon?

Self-doubts persisted in my mind despite my best whack-a-mole efforts to beat them down. We all find ourselves in some kind of fix from time to time, even though some of us are better at faking it, I reasoned to my inner critic, the silent watcher always waiting for a chance to speak up in its ruling of the content of my mind. "Shut up. Shoo! Vanish! Your words are so last year," I admonished. "Get lost! I forgive you for your intrusion, but you're dismissed."

I needed to reorder the emotional chaos in my head for a more positive view of myself. While I would remember this mistake with embarrassment and regret, I acknowledged that its worst consequence would be a delay in getting to the finish line, an unexpected turn off my path. Yes, I grieved as I heard the curtain fall on my hope for achieving the Executor year. I had now lost the upper hand on that possibility. The universe, clearly, had its own plans for things. While we can't predict the future, one thing we can agree on is that it's not likely to go according to plan...at least not when you're new in an endeavour. We are all dynamic beings. We learn as we live. It does hurt to fall on your face this way, but this isn't a disaster. It's a temporary set-back, a little contretemps—my mother's expression during my youth. Perfect or even right conditions rarely exist in life, and I needed to trust in my journey, to let go of that one year goal and focus on the next steps. Nothing to be gained by being angry with myself. I would get there at the right time. With this adjustment in perspective, I was able to create in my head the framework for the evening's tough, face-to-face conversation with the kids.

We left this rather grim banking experience to go to the cemetery for a visit with Marilyn and Richard. I saw her at my side as clear as day and heard her say, "When did you become such a cliché? Standing at a columbarium, consulting the dead, your head full of dark thoughts?"

"I'm here to clear my head," I said. "My Marilyn Project has just taken a sharp detour, and it's entirely my fault." Surrounded by columbaria, I felt the spirits within having fun at my expense, in turn mocking and watching me with stern disapproval, as though bringing my act of omission directly to God's attention.

At eye level with Marilyn's name marker, I shuddered and asked: "What do you think of my work on your behalf in light of today's revealed blunder?"

So she gave me a pep talk. "Why the long face? Chin up. Don't lose heart. Remember, you're a woman with a mission," she said, the voice of solicitude. "Chill out. It's easy to see that a problem like this doesn't amount to a hill of beans in this crazy world." I smile as I heard her say this—her adopted line from one of her all-time favourite movies, *Casablanca*. "You've never been stupid a day in your life, except the times you thought you were. Don't be so hard on yourself and don't let your demons distort what you see. You're getting there. Look on the bright side and give yourself a round of applause for getting this far. There are no mistakes, you know—only the lessons learned along the way. Remember the Chinese Proverb: "Fall down seven times, stand up eight." Executorship, like most things, is best learned by doing."

She told me what I needed to hear. I couldn't have said it better myself, I thought, having trouble holding back the tears. I felt her presence so clear and tangible, I could smell the black bar soap on her skin and was comforted by her booster shot of good advice, the warmth of her hand on my shoulder. This graveyard tête-à-tête was a comforting and peaceful interlude in my day that no longer felt so hard to face. I saw this conversation as a way of living our scheduled telephone visit that never happened.

"This," I told her as I left, "is probably the last time I'll chat with you here, Marilyn. I came really to tell you what I didn't have a chance to say before you left: I loved you very much and you are missed. The memories I carry will live on, but I won't need your columbarium condo to remember that you've always been my greatest cheerleader."

We arrived at Michael and Julia's to be greeted like family, or maybe honoured friends. It was just over a year now since our work together began, and I hadn't seen the kids since our dinner after the reading of the will. It felt like a celebration of sorts, with the ambiance joyful and welcoming. Michael's enthusiastic reception for Bill, especially, was heartwarming. Julia had gone to great lengths to prepare a wholesome meal ready to be served. That in itself was really special because, as a rule, Julia avoided cooking whenever she could. We all enjoyed family updates and the shenanigans of young people in their early twenties over our meal, featuring, of course, the indispensable excellent local wine. Then Michael, Julia, and Jason's girlfriend, Nicole, attended to the dishes while Bill and I sat around the dining room table with Mia, Trevor, and Jason. I looked at these bright faces and was filled with warmth as I thought of Marilyn and how she would live forever through these grandchildren. I wondered if they also thought of it this way.

The room was warm, the lingering smells from dinner contributing to a feeling of comfort and abundance. The atmosphere was one of upbeat anticipation as we began to distribute Marilyn's gifts. These, I learned in my readings, are called bequests, a word that applies equally to personal and household belongings. Distributing bequests is not a tightly scripted exercise but a dynamic human interaction in which surprises can manifest, given all the emotions attached to the recent loss the beneficiaries have experienced. I found it to be an intense time, perhaps one of the best times in the process, and one that requires a degree of humility so that everyone is left feeling good at the end of the day.

We began with the collection of cash and coins. I was grateful for Bill taking over that presentation, since he had done the research and tabulation. Their decision was to leave the collection with Mia, and she would manage its details for the three of them. I then opened the box of beautiful jewellery, possessions of both financial and great sentimental value. Emotions flowed as each piece triggered special memories. Each item had an attached appraisal and the name of one of the three beneficiaries. I felt I was leading someone else's life, channeling Marilyn as I handed out these uniquely precious gifts. The literature advises that as Executor, for my own protection, I should have obtained signed receipts for the bequests I distributed. I confess that I failed to do so. There were, however, five of us around the table witness to and in agreement on every detail of these distributions, so I believed the risk of dissatisfaction was minimal.

There is nothing logical about feelings, I know. Emotions are as individual as the people who own them. To say I was now nervous as we moved to the estate account would be the understatement of understatements. I was sitting in a cold sweat, with the stink of anxiety and the flaming cheeks brought on by profound shame, the shame I felt like a burning ulcer deep in my gut, in my dim view of having failed at an elemental task anyone else would have mastered. I worked to cover up this malaise with the slow retrieval of the file from my briefcase. *Steady*, I told myself. *I've got this.*

Honesty and integrity are absolutely essential for success in the Executor process—a solid foundation, actually, in all areas of life. It's critical to be transparent, objective, and completely above board in this relationship based on trust, and it's never a good idea to run away from or to dance around the truth. That is a true test of character, and how you proceed will reveal the strength of your moral compass. You just can't bargain with the truth or spin self-serving excuses. "If you mess up, fess up" is an essential motto to embrace. Sounds pretty straightforward, right? No genius to it. I was committed to full disclosure with the beneficiaries so invested in the outcome of the process. I believed this to be a practice that makes reciprocity implicit: When you need help, I'll be there for you.

Swallowing my pride and gathering my dignity with both hands, I reiterated with evident poise and confidence, in a calm and respectful voice, what I had emailed them: That my aim today was to close the account and to distribute all the account funds. Today, however, we discovered an unexpected glitch. I made no attempt to sugar-coat the truth. I explained the newly acquired financial information, the requirement to treat the RIF as income in the year of death, and the implications of this finding on the closing of the estate. As I spoke, there wasn't a sound other than my voice in the room. All eyes, bright and alert, were on mine, with full concentration on my every word, gesture, inflection. I saw nods of understanding as I outlined the essential next steps with the clarity and elegance of grace under pressure. No one spoke or even batted and eye as I levelled with them, finishing with the assurance that the right steps had been taken, and while we would be losing some time to complete the settling of the estate, it should otherwise be clear sailing from here. This, I expected, would be the last impediment to completion.

To my great relief, they accepted what in my head was shaped to be this big dramatic reveal as simply part of the process. There was no discomfort or disappointment on their part. They voiced no question or concern. I was reassured to see that they appreciated learning of the next steps and focused their attention not on the one glitch but across the horizon to the finish line. They thanked me wholeheartedly for my work on their behalf and gratefully accepted the cheques I handed them. I accepted these manifestations of support as evidence of the integrity of the process to date and the resulting strength of our partnership, believing that without the first, the second would be unimaginable. We discussed the steps going forward. Once the taxes were paid, we would be in a position to close the account. This wouldn't trigger the need for me to return to Kelowna. I would simply have the bank send them a cheque for the remaining balance.

In closing, I reminded them of two important things:

1. We had received the very important Clearance Certificate from the CRA confirming that there were no outstanding debts owing.

2. The three of them had signed an Executor Release and Indemnity form that had the effect of releasing me from further responsibility following the distribution of the remaining assets in early December—the work we were doing now together. We had the option now of having them take me out of the loop to complete the process themselves if they preferred. They could choose to follow-up directly with the accountant and file for the taxes owing on the RRIF with the CRA. They would distribute the remaining assets amongst the three of them and pay the remaining taxes owing on the RRIF as a final step. This would then put them in a position to close the estate.

Well, they were horrified at the thought of taking this on and asked me to continue to manage the estate to the point of closure. I agreed wholeheartedly, knowing that it would be stressful for them to undertake this challenge at this stage in the process. And the extraordinary thing is that the meeting I had anticipated might be difficult ended with a feeling of complete acceptance and satisfaction. Our time together had been time well spent, and the hours I'd spent on the work were forgotten.

We gathered in the living room, glass of wine in hand, chatting as any group of friends would and joining Michael in his delight over the multiple features, including the picture clarity, of his brand new 62-inch Smart TV. I had worried about Michael and would have loved to chat with him about his feelings and his health, now that a year had passed since his mother's death, but in the midst of this family gathering, the opportunity didn't present itself. I was comforted to see him looking well and certainly cheerful. Perhaps TV therapy had been helpful, I thought with a chuckle. We parted with the promise to keep in touch.

At bedtime, I became moody and introspective as my mind started to dredge up every mistake I ever made, as if they were gathering together to swallow me up. I wallowed in darkness, more than a smidge cranky, as prickly, actually, as my rattail cactus. I had the insight to realize these were the kinds of afterthoughts that plague all Executors as they lay alone in their bed wondering about the "ifs." If only I had known. If only I had. If only...I recognized this as my dark night of the soul and determined to not fall back in the self-made pit of misery that seemed lodged permanently in my thoughts. It's an indulgence, sometimes, to think the worst of ourselves, and it's important to shift to neutral. Despite my wishes, I couldn't let this slide off my shoulders like a strip of Teflon. I wouldn't go off the deep end but strive for coherence and meaning as I reflected on the day's important lesson about the pitfalls of executorship. This was the matter I feared hiding in the background, with the portentous power to take a big juicy bite.

Other than episodes of grief assaulting me from all sides, this was the first real rain on my parade along this, at times, gut-wrenching process. What I was brooding over was deep and hard to admit. Perhaps I went about my role the wrong way. This was an experience that might have been avoided had I kept David's services to handle the entire process. I consoled myself as I landed on the silver lining, the plus side of this equation: Had I kept David's services, I would have had to pay significantly more legal fees. Even if he had decided to use a paralegal for some of the activities, legal services would still be expensive.

I remembered that the source of my initial reluctance to take on the role was fear of not being good enough, and as the same doubt resurfaced, I reminded myself that I'm the one in charge of my own voice, capable of shaping my monologue to one of acceptance and possibility. I just needed to cut myself a little slack, to claim a forgiveness coupon, a strategy used in business these days to encourage staff to take risks. The coupon is a stamped piece of paper that grants permission to make mistakes free and clear, without fear of blame or retribution. Oh well, that might not work in this context. I would tune out this negative voice in my head telling me I made a stupid error, take the learning and run with it, knowing that while at times it's clear that I'm groping in some aspects of the work, it's also true that I don't have to grope alone.

Inexplicably, a picture popped into my head of myself in our farmyard as a child learning to stilt-walk with my brothers. We would fabricate stilts out of old pieces of wood we'd find in the farm and a strip of scrap wire. We'd walk very carefully at first but then learned that it was when we hesitated or stopped that we fell. Eventually, we raced each other to the end of the summer. Now was not the time to stop and fall flat on my nose like the novice stilt-walker I once was. Surrender was not an option. It was full speed ahead. I wouldn't be profiled as a hysterical female known for histrionics who folded under pressure when forced to deal with a less than ideal situation. I would not just cope but take control, hell-bent on getting the job done. Having exhausted my ability to introspect, and feeling marginally better, I closed my eyes on the warmth of my relationship with the beneficiaries, grateful for their thoughtfulness and support along the way. A good night's sleep would help me move beyond the painful memory.

Tuesday, December 4, 2018

Self-nurturing is important after a set-back, and a visit with Jack fell into that category of fun—a wonderful hour of respite. As we sipped our coffee, I asked about the distinct twinkle in his eye and the spring in his step, which prompted him to share his excitement about his Hawaiian lady love expected soon for an extended visit. I was happy for him.

Our time in Kelowna flew by and it was back to the airport to head home. Sadly, there had been no time for a visit with Jody.

Thursday, December 6, 2018

Up with the sun rising on a new winter day, snuggled on the couch, one of my favourite spots in the house, facing the hearth, its fire crackling against the chill of the early morning. Me and my coffee. I hugged my cup, allowing the heat to seep in as I listened to the muted notes of Beethoven's Ninth in the living room. I enjoyed rare mornings such as this when I was up early, thinking in the silence of dawn. My mind wandered in a hundred directions, feeling the residual after-travel fatigue. Looking at the photos taken in Kelowna. Reflecting on the days passed. Making sense of the process, an organic process with no specific formula, an endeavour of methodical discipline with each step completed a small victory.

I asked myself if I were to outline the hallmarks of executor-ship, what that would look like. Having lived the Executor process, I could now bounce the meat and potatoes on my fingertips:

1. Preparing for our eventual demise is difficult but essential and ideally begins long before the end of our life through thoughtful estate planning.

2. Taking the right measures is critical to the successful management of end-of-life health, business, and estate management processes. The right measures include making a will, specifying the appointment of a personal representative through a Representation Agreement, including a "living will" outlining end-of-life care wishes, signing an Enduring Power of Attorney, and appointing a thoughtfully selected Executor. Appointing an alternate for each of these roles is a preferred strategy.

3. There is no standard death and no standard after-death protocol to follow. The will drives the process, keeping the Executor focused on the needs and wants of another. Enough said in these pages about the will. But give it a bold, double asterisk.

4. The gold star for good executorship is for making the most of the legacy for the benefit of the beneficiaries.

5. Executorship is a role worthy of respect and of inspiring fear. Every good journey has good guys and bad guys. The villains in this journey that takes you places that involve peaks and valleys of deep emotions and deep love are Loss and Grief. To sum it up, the greatest hard-ship in the role of Executor is its timing at a time of loss and grief, a time when the emotional turmoil might be immobilizing. Joseph Campbell said, "Find a place inside

where there's joy, and the joy will burn out the pain." The Executor can't afford to let her emotions derail progress and must burn out the pain, perhaps halting it at times, to embrace her duties. Keeping grounded in meaningful life-affirming activities, such as time with grandchildren, will help to maximize health and well-being.

6. Risk is a four-letter word throughout the journey. It casts a shadow with the ever-present potential for latent errors in the chain of events. Doing God's work is not enough. The Executor has to acquire knowledge and exert discipline. Diligence and attention to details are the Executor's best friends. The Executor may skin her knees at times with humiliation along the way and feel the axe over her head, but acknowledging the risks when denial might be a more appealing place to be is helpful in getting back on track. Honesty, even when telling the truth is difficult, will win the day. A willingness to take the risk perhaps leads to becoming the best version of yourself.

7. The language of death is in and of itself is an opportunity for learning along the way. Think probate and ask your friends if they know the word. Think bequest—you get the picture.

8. Now in reflection and in the telling, the process sounds simple, and it's true that many things at first glance appear to be insurmountable yet turn out to be entirely doable. But I do not wish to deceive. Executorship, while it may not be the brainchild of a space engineer, is complex work with a lot of ground to cover in a short time frame. You know what I mean—the pressure cooker effect. While trial-and-error are at times the best teachers in some life scenarios, there's not much room for that in

estate management. The process does not present multiple choice options. It might sound strange to say, but the path is riddled with absolutes, with only one course of action ultimately right or wrong, good or bad. The will and the legislation are the defining guides, yet the pathway isn't a straight line. We all do the Executor role in our own way with creative strategies that are possible to insert between the right way and the wrong way of executorship and with a depth of richness that comes only from first-hand experience, no matter how many hours one might spend poring over reference books. Each estate has its own uniqueness for the Executor to untangle, just as every lock has its own key. The process of untangling is unique to each of us because our life experiences and skills are unique.

9. Much of the Executor's work is solitary work, and the Executor needs to be comfortable flying solo at times. Acceptance of the code of the Canadian Prairie Pioneer is of tremendous help. A day in the life of the Executor looks different every day. This makes it enjoyable, interesting, and rewarding work that is not easily summarized in social situations. Everyone's life situation and estate are unique; therefore, serving as Executor is never twice the same.

10. Relationships with reciprocity are gold in estate management. Of course, relationships take work, but neglect this at your own risk. Sharing of deep feelings will surface at this time perhaps more than at any other. The telling of these personal stories is important even when they hurt, and the Executor is in a great position to serve as a supportive listener. Ongoing communication with the beneficiaries is essential to achieving a good outcome. At

critical points along the way, my people stuck with me, and that made all the difference.

11. Fear in the process of executorship is caused by lack of knowledge of the process steps and the lurking potential for the ambush of irreversible errors. But executorship is not do-it-yourself-brain-surgery. You don't need to have a master's degree or a background of wealth or privilege. You don't have to be dazzling or of a certain age or gender. In other words, and depending on personal circumstances, almost any adult with good preparation and a support team can do the job. If there is another time for me, I will have the confidence of entering the process eyes wide open and knowing where to look for the cracks. I will know the work is challenging but I will have no fear.

In my private life, I am not a loner, but I am often alone, sometimes for weeks at a time, content with my privacy and without the pain of loneliness, so the singular work of estate management generally suited me. Now, however, I was struggling with a subtle feeling I was trying to pin down, and I realized with a deep, visceral, and surprisingly painful knowledge that I was feeling isolated, lonely in this work, a little weary, almost desolate having felt in full measure the impact of the bumps along the road and having seen how with a single decision things can go off the rails very quickly. This, for me, was a new breed of anxiety, subtle and diffuse and stubbornly hovering in the periphery of my consciousness.

I had vented my struggles with my family, of course. They listened, heard, and learned and commiserated with me. I appreciated their support and understanding. It's weird feeling alone when you're surrounded by attentive family. But right now I wanted more. Work in the absence of colleagues was taking a toll on me. I had always worked hand in glove within a strong interdisciplinary team with the shared skills needed to manage all the details. I was now one in a large workforce of solo workers working from home, with irregular hours, with no water cooler or photocopy room or staff lunchroom for shop-talk, or a colleague in the office next door with whom to have an informal check-in. *Even the Lone Ranger had Tonto*, I thought. I craved that collegiality I'd experience at every point in my career, which led me to question whether any professional could thrive without their network. I sighed for all Executors as I thought how nice it would be to have associates, even acquaintances, on a like-minded journey with whom to share a pressing question, chew the fat, discuss issues, share ideas, dole out advice, and hammer home important points. An Executor Café, structured as a peaceful, supportive oasis in the style of Death Cafés, would provide such a milieu. Not a virtual salon but a face-to-face gathering place to connect, a place where diversity of thought and knowledge would de-risk decision-making, a think tank for power thinking on issues of executorship. A community. The more people involved the more valuable the brain thrust would be and greater the potential for the novice to learn the tricks needed to find their way through the work.

Yes, Death Cafés are a thing. Google it if you don't believe me. They're a growing global movement, a death club for conversations over cake and coffee—not to be morbid but to raise awareness and to help people become comfortable with death and their eventual demise, including a focus on grief and on strategies for planning the death details as conscientiously as a person would plan their own daughter's wedding. It may not be everyone's cup of tea, but there aren't many places where talking about death is OK, certainly not around the kitchen table in most families. The Death Café provides that milieu for support and openness on a topic generally held taboo. Similarly, an Executor Café would exist to support people immersed in the process, particularly those who, like me, never settle for being second-rate at anything and are intent on retaining control as opposed to outsourcing the work to lawyers, accountants, and trust companies. Just as a Death Café deprives death of its strangeness, an Executor Café would deprive the role of its mystery and isolation, leading to the reframing of what might be a victim's painful story for some to a hero's journey infused with meaning. Success in this creative process that holds a very slight margin for error, as in any other process, favours the connected, I reasoned, and I felt almost motivated to start such a network.

Perhaps we call the process complicated only because we fear missing a step along the way. As I thought this, knowing that all pieces interconnect in the broadest sense, I felt a deep appreciation for the healing powers of the implicit creativity that is part of the process. Then I noodled over the right words for my role, feeling up to my ears in OPP—Other People's Business—that had become fully mine. Having almost reached the end of the road on my Executor journey, I knew first-hand that this involvement could become a ride with unexpected detours and surprises, and that it brought with it risks you may not be aware of until the end, vulnerability in ways that may not be immediately evident. We all take emotional risks when we try to help others, and managing an estate is no exception to the rule. As I write, I think about my friend who recently discovered, after her brother's death, that she was named Executor of his estate, a large and complex estate. She might have said no had he asked her, but she has taken it on despite the huge drain on her time, energy, and health. Avoiding this kind of scenario with those we love is within our power by simply addressing the topic in open conversation with potential great benefits for a small investment of time and effort.

I mused on the well-known secret of success that applies in this work as in any other: keep your butt in the chair. Stasis is the enemy. This journey is a marathon, not a sprint, and what you choose to do next when you stumble is what really counts. I acknowledged

I've always been driven to do well, always been tough on myself, applying pressure I wouldn't tolerate from anyone else. I finished up with the idea that perhaps these traits explained why life has indeed been very good to me. I concluded that I did the right thing jumping into the fray, but I find that I'm of two minds on the question of would I do it again. The first has to do with the few bruises I've collected along the way. I reason that with my considerable learnings in this experience, I would be primed to avoid the causes in a future similar endeavour. The second is about the irresistible appeal of the expectation of discovery along that journey, the work a path to growth, the feeling almost of a spiritual expansion, something vastly more interesting than the details of my quiet lifestyle. The experience became as much of an adventure as anything else I'd ever undertaken. It served to enrich my life. So yes, hands down, I would do it again—perhaps, you think, this is strong evidence of temporary insanity.

Satisfied with my analysis and my coffee drained, I took my mug to the kitchen. No time to drag-ass. A simple breakfast of toast and cheese for me this morning. I've got work to do.

I was hoping to hear from Irene. Thinking about my accounting work with Val and Irene, all of which was completed by telephone and email, I was deeply thankful for modern day technology, but I regretted not having had the opportunity to meet either in person. I wished I had because they were both worth their weight in gold. I'd emailed Irene the previous day, explaining the RIF experience at the bank. She expressed no surprise, explaining that the federal government regards all assets as disposed of, for tax purposes, as of the time of death. This includes RIFs, with the entire amount remaining in the plan considered income as of the time of death and subject to income tax needing to be filed in that specific year, at which time it is taxed at the marginal rate of the deceased. This means, explained Irene, is that what we needed to file wasn't for 2018 but an adjustment to our 2017 filing. Then came the "Oh, shit" discovery; not only would we have to pay the taxes, but the CRA would impose a fee for late filing.

This new surprise was a great example of how all actions on this journey bring consequences, hence the need to know what you're doing and hope everyone else does as well. *I don't want to encounter any more of these nasty gems*, I thought as it became clear to me that this would be news to Adam as well. He obviously didn't know this, or he would have told me a year ago.

Irene explained that the investment firms and banks don't necessarily have the knowledge to always give their clients the information they need. Their office currently had three clients who had recently had the same experience I was dealing with in the management of their estate. This had put her office on high alert for all their clients.

I appreciated that my difficult experience could be of benefit to others immersed in this complex process.

I heard my email come in and glanced warily at my iPad, fearing more bad news, only to find this gem from Jack:

Re: *Merry Christmas*

> *As we walk through this hi-way of life we encounter certain things that we never would have thought of just a few moments before, such as the case of Marilyn my neighbour and good friend. Never in a million years would I have expected her to pass so quick as she did nor would I ever thought for a moment that through her passing you would enter into our world not just as an acquaintance but as it turned out to become a very dear friend. That alone is a very hard commodity to find in this day and age. Marilyn was very fortunate to have you as a friend - that goes without saying. My family and I feel the same way.*

His words, such simple words, went straight to my heart. In my return email, I told Jack the story about the Ancient Egyptians' beliefs in the afterlife. They believed that by saying the name of a dead person you could make them live forever. He agreed with me that between the two of us we could keep Marilyn from falling into obscurity, if not forever, at least for a very long time.

Monday, December 10

Email from Adam:

Re: *The T4*

> *The T4 for the RIF will be issued early in the New Year.*

20

—

Lightness of Joy

I'm a shopper, like everyone else I know, at Christmastime but not one to have my shopping finished by Thanksgiving. It was getting a bit late in the season, so I treated myself to a day at St. Vital Mall, planning to finish my purchases, or at least the gifts for my grandchildren. I wouldn't see Christmas spoiled for the kids, however crowded my mind was with estate matters. My mood was up and steady, and I even looked forward to braving the crowded madness at the mall. As soon as I got there, however, I stumbled across a Palliative Manitoba Program intended to help ease the pain of grief during the holiday season. It offers a beautiful ritual that invites you in a uniquely individual way to mark your loss and your love, an opportunity for catharsis, a means to perhaps even grow in your journey with grief; a sort of way-station between grief that clings to you like a shadow and letting go when saying goodbye is hard to do.

I found the idea compelling because the need and desire to acknowledge those we love runs deep in most people, and it's only human to nurture a connection with loved ones, even after they've passed away. This was a new program to me, and I appreciated its intent instantly, recognizing that grief can be a constant companion on a long journey, not something you have at a certain point and you're done. Anyone who wishes to participate is invited to write a message on a card as a tangible way to remember and acknowledge a loved one who has died. The card is then hung, like a treasured ornament, on an enormous Christmas tree, a Memory Tree, softly lit with classic warm white LED lights and prominently displayed right where you can't miss it, in front of the entrance to The Bay.

The tree soared, its every branch and bough full of cards from the bottom up, including a number of very distinctive children's cards. Plenty of art supplies were available for the kids to work with. A volunteer explained the program to me, and I was left with the impression that their training and dedicated support must be of great benefit, especially for the participating kids and their parents.

The poetic symbolism in this approach and the vehicle it presents to express a state of mind appealed to me. As I sat down to write, I thought of Michael, wishing he were here to write a note, because sometimes the most important things are the hardest things to say in person.

My words are wont to skip out of reach at times when my emotions are high, and my mind was now momentarily blank.

"There's no need to rush," said the volunteer with whom I'd been chatting. "Take your time."

I took out my Mont Blanc, and because I had no clear idea of where to start, I simply began to write:

"Hello, Marilyn. Monday would have been our scheduled telephone call. I miss you and wish my smart phone was smart enough to reach you now so we could chat one more time. Your coordinates are still in my data base, and I'm caught by surprise, and then I send you a hello, every time I tap in an M and your name pops up. You were gone before I knew it, leaving no chance for a proper goodbye. I can't write in this brief note all the things I didn't have a chance to say. I'm a bit at a loss for words anyway, but let me ask you this question: Do you remember the day we first met?

"That's where our story started in 1967. You knew my name before I walked into the nursing station with all the nervous anticipation of a rookie. You didn't shake but held my hand as you said good morning. Then you introduced me to everyone and said, 'Welcome to the team. We make music here together,' and we all went in, laughing, to shift change report for the scoop on our patients and for our assignments. Then Willy gave me an orientation to the unit, introducing me to the patients we met on our walk- about. Don't think we didn't all know Willy was your favourite. And we all cried together when cancer claimed him as a young man, leaving behind his wife and little boy."

As the memories unwound, I remembered thinking then that I already knew those people, and working there would not only be a joy but a privilege. I didn't know it then, but I learned over years of experience that when a nursing unit works like that one, there's a strong head nurse (whatever the contemporary name for that role is) at the helm, and I could feel the force of her personality in every detail, including the daily patient assignments.

"Some days I think you've left, but all I have to think about is my time on this unit and I'm transported back across decades with you right there beside me—on this unit that was yours as surely as if you had designed, built, decorated, and furnished it yourself. Thank you for this experience that served as a strong foundation for my entire career. I thought you were nuts, by the way, when you gave up your job to move to B.C. Then I was filled with admiration at your courage when you opened up a group home in Kelowna for young men with schizophrenia recently discharged from hospital. Your initiative improved their health prospects significantly as well as facilitating their successful integration in the community. I didn't know you had the entrepreneurial savoir-faire for this. It was a great surprise, and I felt a bit envious because it seemed at the time that your days were so much more exciting than mine, immersed in hospital settings. Please know that your investment in those with mental illness contributed to advances in the field. Your life mattered. Have a Merry Christmas wherever you are. You will be remembered.

Love,

Gm"

My gratitude felt overwhelming, and I was flooded by warm thoughts as I travelled back in time uncovering precious recollections.

"Thank you for so much more," I wrote on a second card, and then a third, which I stapled inside the first. "The weekends at the lake, the feasts of saffron rice and gingered ribs baked on slow and low for unparalleled tenderness, the rum punch, the laughter over stories told in the dark around the fire pit, our conversations kept light over cups of coffee and ginger snaps. For trusting me to serve as your Maid of Honour. The open arms for my family on all our trips to B.C. Thank you for rocking my babies. For your support when my daughter had cancer, and for walking with me when times were tough. For your follow through in the gun-held-to-my-head incident that turned my life upside down. Your support was instrumental to my recovery. Thank you for your love and generosity over years of friendship. You will always be a part of me."

You might think I'm a weird old lady as I tell you this, but I saw her sitting beside me right there under the Christmas tree while I wrote two full pages plus. It's OK if you do. I'm well passed the stage in my life in which being considered weird brings a stab of inferiority and shame. I felt good sitting there by her side. She also goaded me to write as I chuckled and looked her in the eye:

"But no thanks for appointing me as the Executor of your estate. No hard feelings. Don't come back to haunt me."

I folded and taped my bulging card and placed it as high as I could reach on the tree. Then I went home, no longer in the mood to browse. Stepping in the lightness of joy, I felt my grief lifting. I left behind the hollow sadness, the burden that had weighed me down.

This program, apparently well-known and popular in Winnipeg, has been running during the month of December since 1987. It's no surprise that the program has wide appeal, because everyone has experienced loss at some point. Everyone. At the end of the event, the tree is dismantled, and the cards are collected for a card burning ceremony called Light the Memories, an offering to the gods as the words are symbolically released into the sky. This event takes place as a popular social gathering in Assiniboine Park in the spring. The park is very beautiful, so I might go. Maybe.

On the same day, Canada Post brought me a Christmas card from Julia, speaking also on behalf of Michael and the kids, with seasonal good wishes and words of thanks for my work on the estate. I was thrilled with this as a tangible and lovely gift in these days of mostly email messages. Enclosed was a Starbucks gift card. Touched that she remembered my love of a good latte, I felt blessed in that moment and wished for nothing more. I sent her a virtual hug to pass on to Michael and the kids.

21

February 6, 2019

—

Keeping Grounded

I had sent a document I'd received from Germany to Irene, four long pages entirely in German. Fortunately, Irene's colleague, Elizabeth, another angel I never met, is fluent in German and had for years looked after Marilyn's German account. From her translation, we knew that this document was a bill from the German tax department claiming taxes owing, of course, in Euros. Thankfully, there were no arrears, and it was a small amount. Marilyn paid her taxes responsibly. I connected Adam with Irene, hoping the bank could send a wire transfer. Turned out the bank couldn't do a wire transfer, but they could do a Euro draft. I signed the authorization form, and this is what we sent to Germany to complete the payment. I chided myself, once again, for having overlooked the likelihood that there would be taxes to pay to Germany, given the evidence of this annual process in the stack of tax returns, the goldmine of information in my pink zippered bag. Accustomed to the Canadian system, I had been blind to this element of her estate management. If there was ever a next time, I would now know better.

I was growing tired of the Prairie winter and happy that the days were getting longer with spring on the horizon. More importantly, we were now into March, and I still hadn't received the T4 I needed. Adam assured me he hadn't seen it either and encouraged patience. Finally, on March 22, the long-awaited T4 showed up on Marilyn's CRA account. We had all the information we needed to proceed; however, the accounting firm was extremely busy, as all accounting firms are at that time of year processing their clients' taxes. Irene apologized for the delay as she told me they would proceed with filing the T1 adjustment in May. I was impatient, but again there wasn't much I could do but wait.

April 13, 2019

At this stage in my life, the years, like New Year's resolutions, disappear quickly with one season rushing into another, no matter how we might wish time would stand still for a bit. Of course, I would have said the same thing when I was 25. Still, we'd just had Christmas, and now it was my daughter's birthday. Next week we'd be celebrating Easter and skipping outdoors, happy to have shed the constricting winter clothing. Then before we knew it, we'd be sweltering in the humid Winnipeg summer and enjoying long days when it stays light until way past my bedtime. The passage of time is a mystery, and without the love of family and friends, each day would bring a great deal of loneliness. Every moment has to be savoured and lived to the fullest.

Life is more than work, I reminded myself, recognizing my tendency to measure time by the next check mark on my task list. I made a point of making sure the Executor eased off so the woman could relax and trade off the work for an enjoyable distraction, a chance to regroup and replenish, to clear her mind. My days with

Noah created such a distraction and centred my life in important ways, including pulling me out of episodes of grief. I was reminded of the importance of play even when the work isn't finished.

So we take our fun seriously, and every day we have Noah's Academy built into our schedule. Noah, the boy who it seems like just yesterday was toddling around my coffee table learning to walk, is my yoga master, my miniature yogi with oversized paws. His teacher, Brianna, teaches the kids yoga in his daycare centre. I often send her silent thanks for her wisdom in recognizing that kids can benefit from practising yoga as much as adults do. We rolled out our mats, mine a dull burgundy, his appropriately decorated at each end with a large lime green monkey in a playful pose.

"First, you take a deep breath," he said, breathing in deeply to demonstrate, "right down to your tummy button. And if you have a weakness, remember to try to protect it. Do you have a weakness, Grammia?" This was his name for me when he was learning to talk, and it stuck.

"Yes, my bladder is weak."

"What's a bladder?"

"It's a little pouch in our tummies that holds pee."

"Oh, you mean your penis."

Then, with utmost confidence, great calm, and his face bright with the sheer joy of it, he began the class with the happy baby pose, clearly his favourite. He waited for me to do my pathetic version of it before moving into a tree pose.

"Now you have to make the sounds with me, Grammia."

I heard the hiss and saw the snake in front of me, followed by a yawning hippo and then the soft hum of a giraffe. He then easily adjusted his limbs once more in the manner of a circus contortionist, limber as our monkey ancestors, into the ferocious roar of a charging lion. I repeated each move, sounding like ancient, rusty hinges in my efforts to twist my body into what felt tighter than a red licorice Twizzler. At one point I was laboriously trying not to wobble while standing on one leg to master the barking dog pose and wagging my leg like a dog's tail. Just when I thought I had it right, he stopped in mid-pose and said, "Don't worry, I'll position you." He ran over to adjust my arm and leg to his exact understanding of perfection. A few more poses and we were done for that Academy day. I put together my prayer hands and said a humble "Namaste." He looked at me with his eyes the colour of melted chocolate and, mimicking my posture and tone of voice, he said, "Poo." No surprise. The favourite word of a four-year old. Then he laughed—not a tentative laugh, but a wholehearted explosion from his little boy gut that filled the living room with joy and sent my shoulders shaking on the floor. The intended effect of yoga relaxation came with the laughter, and I felt a state of profound well-being wash over me. I would have stayed right there on the floor for the next hour, but Noah's laughter was over a mere moment after it began.

Catching himself as if he'd forgotten something important, he stood on the couch, placed his right hand on his heart with a look sweet enough to charm the very stars from the blue sky, and sang in a pure and solemn, angelic voice:

The sun goes down
The stars come out
All that counts is the here and now
My universe will never be the same
I'm glad you came
I'm glad you came

His bottomless capacity for joy buoyed my spirits, and as my happiness quotient spiked, my eyes grew misty in the moment of pure Zen. I'm sure the Wanted weren't thinking of children's yoga with their composition, but in my view, it's a perfect context. The kids benefit in so many ways and share their love.

The Noah's Academy performances, with modified sequences each week as he learned new poses, have etched themselves among my cherished memories. While they were simply too much fun to place me in a solid meditative state, they did serve to root me in a state of mindfulness, my mind sparkling with remarkable clarity acutely aware of our shared energy and feeling the privilege of this exceptional experience, which I came to understand as a ritual of spiritual practise marked by awareness and intention. There's quite a buzz these days about mindfulness, its benefits having been tested and verified. Even the corporate world has embraced its demonstrated value to enhance performance and spur creativity. Business could, I figure, benefit from Noah in the role of consultant.

Some days, chaos is the operative word in our home, but boredom has no place anywhere in our vocabulary. After Noah's Academy, we transitioned to our daily Grammia's Academy and snuggled on the couch for today's reading: *The Gruffalo.* I stroked his head gently as I read, breathing in the scent of my little yogi's hair.

* * *

We've closed on a year now since receiving the Grant of Probate. Despite my best intentions and ferocious discipline, finishing my Marilyn Project still hovers like a mirage in the distance. Some mornings I wake up and it hits me: I still have work to do. So I reach for my notebook for the day's tasks.

Saturday, April 28, 2019

Email to beneficiaries:

> Re: *Estate Update:*
>
> *"You must be thinking I've forgotten you, but no, I'm still working on the estate. The work, I think, is almost done. Here's what's happening:*
>
> *Shortly after I came home from Kelowna in December, a letter arrived from the CRA equivalent in Germany. Imagine this—it was all in German and I had no clue what it said. Fortunately, Marilyn's accounting firm has a German woman on staff who worked with Marilyn over several years. So I sent her the four-page, 8 X 11 document. It turns out there were taxes owing—just under $1,000.00. It took quite a while to sort it all out and to coordinate with the bank and the accounting firm to send the money to Germany. All done with that now.*
>
> *As we discussed, the RIF should, by law, have been closed at the time of Marilyn's death with the tax implications addressed in the 2017 tax year. This is causing a delay since we're having to file an adjustment to the 2017 tax return. This will be processed in early May. So we're close to the end of the tasks but not quite there yet. I'm sure you're as eager as I am to be finished with all these details. To be continued...I will keep you in the loop.*

Saturday, May 5, 2019

Surprise! Another letter from Germany to my frustration and increasing concern. I wasn't expecting this. With translation we found out that it was a repeat of the previous request but in an entirely different format—a notice to pay the sum we'd already paid. Fortunately, Irene had sent the draft by registered mail and had the receipt. The mail system was slow indeed. Irene called Canada Post, and their agent put in a service request for their international team to track where this item was in their system. That tracking, by the way, could take five business days. We could have avoided this problem by wiring the funds. Too bad the bank wasn't set up for that kind of transfer.

Tuesday, May 8, 2019

The paperwork was completed, and I was celebrating despite the information from Irene that it could take up to eight weeks for a T1 Adjust to be processed. So we'd wait for the Notice of Re-Assessment and expect a penalty for late filing plus interest on the amount. One more thing to worry about: Did we leave enough money in the account?

Monday, June 18, 2019

Email to beneficiaries:

Re: *Estate Update*

Hello, everyone. You must be wondering what's happening. Well, so am I, really. Still awaiting confirmation from the German Government that they have received our tax payment. This is taking a very long time, since the draft was sent three months ago. In the meantime, they keep sending letters of reminder. Totally frustrating!

We are also awaiting a response from the CRA on the tax adjustment. Please note the taxes owing, in addition to what we paid to Germany, will likely take up all of the funds remaining in the account.

I will send you a full account as soon as I hear from these two sources. In the meantime, thank you for your patience.

Tuesday, June 19, 2019

Email reply from Julia:

Thanks for the update. I hope you're having a relaxing summer and not spending all your time working on this. Those darn taxes!!!

Saturday, July 7, 2019

My patience was frayed. Still no word from the CRA. I simply couldn't wait any longer. I called them. Irene was absolutely right—they are very slow with their processing of T1 Adjusts. The staff member I spoke with assured me these were not top priority for them. He could not tell me how much longer it would take. Maybe a couple more weeks. Yikes!

I decided to explore their process further with him while I had him on the phone. He told me that their practice is to bill the beneficiaries directly on these taxes owing. I explained our situation to him and that I was still managing the estate account, so it would make sense for them to bill me as the Executor. His response was that they have no flexibility on this practice regardless of my explanation or my attempts to press him to bill me for it. He emphasized their lack of flexibility in this regard and insisted that they could make no exception.

It seemed clear that I was left with only one option with the estate account: to distribute the remaining funds to the beneficiaries so they would have the dollars before getting the nasty bill from the CRA. Still, I wanted to sleep on this decision...perhaps a premonition of things to come.

Saturday, July 14, 2019

Email to the beneficiaries

Re: *Estate Update*

*Adam will distribute the balance in the estate account in
equal amounts to the three of you as beneficiaries. The
account will then be closed. Watch your mailbox for the draft.*

And with this, really, my work was done. Well, maybe not
quite yet.

Sunday, July 22, 2019

Confirmation received from Germany. Our envelope had finally
reached its destination. Woohoo! Not bad—it only took five
months and sixteen days, many letters to agonize over and trans-
late, Irene's time in the accounting office, Canada Post's tracking,
updates to the beneficiaries, and who knows about the processes
in Germany. No one knows for sure, but it seemed that there
was no need to obtain a clearance certificate from the German
Government as we do with the Canada Revenue Agency. Their
confirmation of funds received will suffice. I was just glad this one
was done. I closed that file.

22

Sunday, August 19, 2019

—

CRA Betrayal

I rose early, indulged in a long bath scented with my favourite bath oil and, still in vacation mode, crafted the very best plan for the day. I would pamper myself with no plans whatsoever. I revelled in the appeal of a day of indulgence, a wholesome breakfast, and getting the mail left to accumulate while we were away and in which I hoped there might be something interesting. The mailbox was jammed full as I expected, and jumping out of the stack was a letter from the CRA. "Why is the CRA sending me a letter?" I wondered, like a true paranoid, as I reached for the letter opener. It can't be good. A letter from the CRA, I've learned over time, never brings good news. In fact, it's more likely to bring pressure for immediate action. And this one certainly was as expected. I moaned as my belly sank to my knees and I felt my heart stop for three full beats. There was no sidestepping the letter's unwelcome significance. It pulled not only the rug from under my feet but the whole floor, suddenly leaving me with no solid ground.

"Merde," I bellowed. My voice rose, along with my anger, in a torrent of abuse in my immediate and fully justified hostility toward the CRA, a mouthful of more profane curses that I dare not list here. I let go a string of rather handsome invectives from the ample French vocabulary developed in my childhood and rarely used since. French swear words have so much more impact: short, rude, and to the point in my mother tongue. Profanities weren't allowed in my home. In fact, I was disciplined to not raise my voice in vulgar signs of temper. I'm telling you, I never learned to swear with such admirable expertise there, even in the backyard games growing up with my rough and tough eight brothers. But I absorbed my share, starting in my elementary school. I wanted to hurl every one of them now with zing as I exploded with the fury I believed I was fully entitled to. My temper was on full boil. I won't deny it or apologize for it. Like everyone else, I'm entitled to drop an F-bomb equivalent at the appropriate time and in whatever language I choose. I crushed the envelope and threw it across the room but with little satisfaction. You've got to be kidding me! Or, in more contemporary language, what the f**k happened?

I had reacted strongly to the first matter as one of great importance that stymied progress toward my Executor year goal, but this matter, by contrast, was ghastly. I didn't deserve to take this one on the chin. I had been strong, practical, and assertive at tough times in my demanding work portfolios, demonstrating stamina, endurance, and resourcefulness but not aggression as a rule. I had felt hurt at times, absolutely, but could think of little in my life that had the power to bring me to this level of all-consuming, bootless rage, to stop me dead in my tracks where restraint and control hovered as vague, unimportant concepts.

It pains me, truly, to trash-talk the CRA with words that are not easily translated and might even frighten the French. Perhaps I should keep my thoughts about the CRA to myself, but this was a complete and, in my view, irresponsible CRA betrayal! Treachery beyond the pale! Sucks to be me! In case you think I exaggerate the risks and pitfalls implicit in the Executor role, consider this scenario: Here I was with a $10,000 bill and no money at my disposal, since the estate account was closed at a time we all believed was the logical and right time. This was not chicken feed. I couldn't ignore this or make it go away with a mouthful of colourful curses. Should I call and blast the CRA as I longed to do? That had a certain appeal, but I cast it aside, believing I would be wasting my breath delivering a rebuke that wouldn't be heard. It would be a battle even David would lose. No one I've ever met wants to tangle with the CRA.

I cursed myself for being an idiot and not making notes of the date, the time, and the name of the person I had spoken with at the CRA. That was a mistake in my process. It had simply never occurred to me that I would be handicapped without that information. It went against the grain for me to retreat in the face of adversity, but I reminded myself of the old saying: "Honey catches more flies than vinegar." Perhaps some finesse would trigger a reversal of their process. Should I call and, using diplomacy and tact and my inside voice, ask them to reverse their approach? To what end? They held all the cards. I felt quite impotent, anticipating defensiveness and not sympathy and yet another process delay. I believed they would not give an inch given their assertions of the inflexibility in their process. Might there be a better solution? I wondered, experiencing the full meaning of pressure.

Oh, did I mention that I was furious with the CRA? Connect the dots and you'll get the picture; it doesn't take a brainiac to see that this ambush by the CRA had the effect of leaving me weak with an open-ended vulnerability and unsettled anxiety. I felt the helpless posture of the novice confronted by the master. "Good Lord!" I said. And I meant it, sending a prayer to whatever gods were listening. Could I Hail Mary my way out of this mess? Probably not. I'm sure I looked completely unhinged as I paced, bare feet slapping the gleaming hardwood floor corner to corner through all the hallways in my home. I wondered if I would ever breathe normally again.

I ordered myself to level, to shake off my anger through movement and distraction, a strategy that usually worked well for me. I felt waist-deep in quicksand, and the rope that bailed me out was my belief in the integrity of the three young people on whose behalf I had been doing this work. As I took a deep, cleansing breath, the voice at the back of my head said, "You can trust these three to do the responsible thing and come through with their share of the money." Still, I confess to a few hours of an emotionally wrenching slog that (spoiler alert) turned out to be needless worry but will remain a memory forever etched into my brain.

The same voice said, "Here's what you should do next." My action plan became simple and clear as I clawed my way back to reason. The force of the fury boiling in me just moments before dissipated. Setting aside my sense of injustice while drawing resources from my private source of wisdom, I found solid ground. I wiped the sweaty palms of my hands on my pant legs, and with my head held high, a habit that suited me well, I went in search of my iPad. Time to call in the reserves. I paused a moment, wanting to make sure I sent the right message.

Email to Jason, Mia, and Trevor (cc. Julia and Michael)

Re: *Taxes Owing*

Hello everyone.

Surprises never end. The CRA assured me that they could not send me the notice of reassessment, that they were completely inflexible in their practice with this process, even as I was very assertive and held my ground on the wisdom of having them send the invoice to me. They insisted they could not make an exception. Their protocol dictates that they must bill the three beneficiaries separately, as per their standard practice (and despite my arguments with them). Guess what... they sent me the notice, which I received in today's mail.

You'll note on the attached that I have to pay the amount by August 29. They will charge interest if the invoice is not paid by then. Judging by the date, this letter probably arrived last week, but I was away, not expecting this, traipsing across the Prairies for a three-week vacation with my family.

As you'll see from the calculation on the notice I've attached, the amount for each of you is $3,404. I'm counting on you to send me a cheque for your amount asap, since we need to pay this right away. Thank you for your help with this necessary step.

Then I crashed on the couch, thinking a glass of wine before dinner was called for. No, make that a double whisky on ice.

Same evening return email from Trevor:

Ok to send you an interact E-transfer?

Of course, Trevor! Thanks. This is such an efficient way to send money, I emailed back, copying all three.

I laughed at myself. The fact that this payment mode was not my first suggestion was strong evidence of my old-fashioned tendencies despite the reality that online banking had changed my life over the last few years. It reflected the very large gap between their ages and mine. Oh well, I reasoned, that highlights the importance of teams ideally having people of all ages.

Crisis resolved. By the next day, all three had sent in their money. Wow! That's what I'm talking about. I felt pure delight; like a million dollars after taxes. *This was truly the high point not just of my day but of my entire Executor journey*, I thought as I let out a quiet, relieved breath. I would hold fast to this happy memory. I knew I'd hit the jackpot with this specific family for my first experience in the Executor role. I had, with good reason, grown to love, respect, and highly value the support of these five individuals I came to call indispensable members of my team, and all the efforts at nurturing this relationship with respectful and clear communication had paid off. Now I dwelled once again on how fortunate I was with this quality of friendship and loyalty as a precious gift.

Monday, August 20, 2019

Email to Jason, Mia, and Trevor (cc. Julia and Michael)

Re: *A Big Thank You*

Hello Jason, Mia, and Trevor. I so very much want you to know how impressed I am with your immediate responsiveness to my request. I am overcome with gratitude. You are so conscientious and so amazing! I love you for it.

I have sent in the payment to the CRA, so I believe we are truly done now. For real!

I'm happy that all the details are looked after, but I'm also sad because I have really enjoyed working with you. And that goes for you too, Michael and Julia.

I hope to hear from you from time to time, perhaps with the highlights in your life. I wish you all the best life can bring.

Au revoir and thanks again.

Response email from Julia:

> *Hi Germaine. Thanks for taking care of all this for the kids and for Marilyn. She was lucky to have you. Hope you are doing well; let us know if you are back in town sometime.*

23

—

Closing the Books

And just like that, with no more fanfare, not with a bang but with the whisper of direct deposits, the estate was settled with the assets distributed as directed by the will. My Executor journey that morphed into a personal quest and near obsession, a pilgrimage, was over.

Mine is a small story. I know that. I haven't witnessed or accomplished the extraordinary. I haven't climbed to a mountain top, completed a marathon, or crossed a hot desert all on my own. I didn't find a cure for cancer or schizophrenia. But I did push at limits, set aside my doubts, and take a risk, stepping up to the plate and honouring what I believe is important in life. And I lived to tell the tale. So it may not be a tour de force, but this is my story, albeit only one of my many stories. I own it; therefore, it matters.

A short time ago, I came from a place of limiting beliefs about my capacity as well as ignorance on the important process of settling an estate. I had a kick-at-the-can and gathered a great deal

245

of knowledge and skills to add to my bag of tricks. Good thing for an old dog! The experience became mine in full measure, not just something that happened to me. It left me with a satisfying sense of aliveness, of completion, of accomplishment so intense I was floating. I was a novice on this round, but now I can tell you with a degree of confidence: "I've lost my green, and with this experience under my belt I'm more than willing to repeat the process."

The journey I walked had a purpose, and what I learned along the way shapes who I am and carries weight—the secret to making a life extraordinary. As we get older and loss becomes more and more a component of an ordinary life, we might as well all pay attention to hear each other's truths and hold each other's hand as we share our learnings. Journeys have greater worth with some complications thrown in the mix.

Serving as Executor, I've come to believe, is a higher calling. I didn't do it for the money. The prize I allowed myself was the learning along the way. Time is not a renewable resource, but for every moment of my time devoted to completing the Executor tasks, Marilyn unknowingly paid me back. Her currency was learning, skill-development, and a feeling of great accomplishment, leaving me feeling more like my executive self, out of retirement. I have re-invented myself, as they say. Through the process, I also realized fully that while preparing a will is the foundation of building an estate plan, there is so much more to think about—strategies and techniques I need to pay attention to in my own financial affairs portfolio and end-of-life details.

When death knocks on your door, there's a whole lot of stuff that needs to be done, but there's this other part that's relational and emotional and spiritual. I feel humble as I reflect on the list of great people I worked with on my journey. These people interactions were, without doubt, the best part, my favourite part, of the process.

Was I a model Executor? Perhaps not. On reflection and in private, I admit that I coloured outside the chalk lines at times, but doing a good job isn't something I took lightly. Now that my experience is in the rear-view mirror, I know that the role of Executor is learned largely through experience and sometimes with humiliation along the way. And while I lost confidence in myself on occasion, I was also tenacious in seeking solutions, as well as bold in my decisions. While I wasn't entirely in control of the complexities lurking within the role at times, and I think any other flaw might be easier to admit, I now see my Executor work as a way of working through my own sense of loss—my grieving cloth. I shake my head as I realize the emotions, and dealing with them, is a big factor I neglected to include in any of my plans. Looking back, however, I'm glad I accepted the executorship. I will not lose sight of how privileged I was to have had this journey. "Yes" was indeed the best answer, even if the call came at a time when a "no" might have made life a lot easier to manage.

I didn't quite make the Executor year, I reflect as I close my files. Whoop-de-do, eh? Speed is not your friend in this process, and the bottom line is that the path is not laid out with all the kinks ironed out. I spent not quite two years in total, one year and four months post probate, on this work. I could give you the hours, the minutes, and seconds, but then you'd think I'm obsessive. The work could have been wrapped up much earlier if not for unexpected delays. The RIF was the proverbial fly in the ointment. I would have made the one-year post probate goal with time to spare if not for that glitch. Regardless, I believe that the Executor year definition is likely too narrow for most estates, since it's hard to gain an edge with so many factors out of the Executor's control. It probably needs redefinition or should be taken with a grain of salt, as the saying goes.

The experience of executorship is meaningful because it's a story with an ending that truly matters. Closing the books brought an undeniable mix of pain and pleasure, but in the final analysis, we did have a happy ending. The experience gave me something I wasn't even aware I'd been looking for: a reminder of my productivity before retirement. I left behind the emotional numbness that was beginning to envelop me and am now ready for the next adventure. Yes, I hit the wall at one point, but none of that matters now that I can bask in the afterglow. I can look back unashamed, unafraid, undeterred. The legacy Marilyn left for her beloved grandchildren was maximized, a testament to the oath I took at the outset. Ahh, the sweet smell of success. It's tough to argue with stellar results. On this thought, a sense of relief beyond words, of perhaps irrational exuberance, washed over me, as if the stressful trials and tribulations along the journey had made the experience that much more poignant. Real life, it seems, can be simultaneously difficult and exciting.

I stashed my fat, bulging binder in my bookcase. *Maybe it sounds like a king-size boast, and my ego may be noticeably bigger*, I thought as I patted myself on the back with a bit of a swagger. But so what? I did a great job, if I do say so myself, and I do, as much in defense as in triumph. I can say my time hasn't been wasted, and that's enough to justify my existence. I acknowledge it was a tough personal journey, but I faced the music and nailed this! Three cheers for me. It's time to celebrate. First, I popped open a full-bodied Okanagan Merlot, raised the glass in a toast, and drank deeply while executing a perfect metaphorical backflip. Then I put on an imaginary bright pink, embroidered and sequined superhero cape in a single-handed flourish. I rang the bell with a shout of "Hallelujah" as I crossed the finish line and wrapped a gold medal around my neck, all of it just to make Marilyn laugh. Then I stepped into the dance of joy with reckless abandon, laughing with her in this moment of perfect joy.

Author's Note

—

This book began when it was too cold to go outdoors. On this Winnipeg winter day it was -30 and the wind was blowing hard. I sat by my fireplace and started writing with no specific audience in mind, feeling a driving need to sort out the events of my experience, even if only for myself. I saw the writing as a hobby, a discipline to exercise my brain outside of its comfort zone, to ponder my experience for a firmer grasp of the language of death and a greater understanding of the mystery of the end-of-life with all its pre- and post-implications. Within a week, the first chapter was done, structured in a fiction format. As the story unfolded, however, I realized I trusted my personal experience and wanted to share with the world my own personal journey, to present a road map of sorts, borne of what I came to see as a unique and special experience that most people would find challenging.

This journey addresses several themes—death, loss, compassion, the power of relationships, courage, self-discovery, problem-solving, skill development, and the healing power of creativity within restrictive parameters. Of course, nobody appointed me the Boss of Executorship, but I took a chance on presenting my point of view on the demanding role of executorship despite the fact that certain parts of my journey were painful to acknowledge in the privacy of my own mind, never mind on a page for public view. There was no right or wrong way to tell the story, but I soon abandoned fiction, feeling pulled toward the personal approach of a memoir. This is my first foray into memoir writing—a work, as I see it, that may not be polished but finished enough for my successes and failures to speak to readers and add insights to their own similar but different journey.

I am a retiree after a 50-year career in health care marked with accomplishments in bedside nursing, teaching, research, consulting, management, administration, coaching, and governance. I have had many roles: a psychiatric nurse in a large psychiatric hospital and general hospital psychiatric units, a registered nurse on medical units, a teacher in hospital-based nursing programs, a head nurse and program manager, a student of public health and health services administration, a consultant in government, a CEO in hospital and community settings, an executive coach, and an avid believer in the importance of good governance with appointments on several Boards of Directors. And I can say truly that I loved every day of my career.

I am also the daughter of Francophone pioneers in the isolated regions of Peace River, Alberta, the daughter of farmers and one of 13 siblings. I am a wife, the mother of two children, the mother-in-law of their spouses, grandmaman of their children, and an active volunteer in my community.

I write to embrace life's offerings twice: in the moment and in the retrospection. It may sound lame, but what I know to be true is that the experience of executorship and its documentation in this book became my grieving cloth. It allowed my body to uncurl from the weight of its emotional turmoil. It brought me home to myself, a gift I didn't expect at the outset.

I have attempted to bring all of these perspectives to bear on what I have written here. But more than anything, this book comes from what I experienced, struggled with, learned, and accomplished in my experience as Executor. Throughout I've sought to express not just the process but also the emotions experienced while immersed in this role. I'm certain of one sure thing: This book arises from the quality of my friendship with Marilyn and from her encouragement and constant support for my development. It comes from her awareness of my skills and her frequently expressed congratulations on my successes.

What would she like to be remembered for? Her devotion to those with mental illness and her commitment to her grandchildren are impressive. She has left me a considerable legacy in so many ways, including the meat of the matter for this book.

As an expression of gratitude for everyone involved in this journey, the names throughout the book have been changed in an effort to protect individual privacy. The dialogue may not be verbatim throughout but rather a paraphrase of real conversations, re-created to the best of my ability to retain the meaning of the exchange.

Resources

—

There is little, I believe, that can't be learned if you have access to an adequate reference library. My solitary nature and lifelong love of books and scholarly study make research generally interesting for me. I have been known to do it just for fun—yes, I am more than a bit weird. In this case, I had to spend a considerable amount of time and use my best finding-out skills to discover, at a very demanding time in my life, the information I needed to flesh out my Executor role. I'm thinking you may not want to spend hours of precious time in your remaining days on earth searching for resources on estate management. With this in mind, I've enclosed the following materials for your ease of reference.

Beattie, Andrew. (2020). "The Executor Checklist: 7 Tasks Before They Die." *Investopedia.* https://www.investopedia.com/articles/retirement/11/executors- checklist-7-things-before-they-die.asp, accessed February 15, 2021.

Beattie, Andrew. (2020). "5 Things to Consider Before Becoming an Estate Executor." *Investopedia.* https://www.investopedia.com/articles/pf/11/before-becoming-an-executor.asp, accessed February 15, 2021/

Berkeley, Benjamin H. (2007). *The Complete Executor's Handbook: A Step by Step Guide for Executors and Personal Representatives*. Sphinx Publishing.

Biscottis, Lynn. (2015). *The Boomers Retire: A Guide for Financial Advisors and Their Clients*, 4th Edition. Toronto: Carswell.

Carter, Thomas G. (2015). *So You've Been Appointed Executor*. Vancouver: Self- Counsel Press.

CIBC Private Wealth Management. (2013). "Duties of an Executor—Estate Administration Responsibilities."

Duncan, Garry R. and Duncan, Andrew G. (2018). *When I Die: Financial Planning for Life and Death*. Toronto: Thompson Reuters.

"Executor/Liquidator Kit for Settling an Estate." https://ca.rbcwealthmanagement.com/documents/659077/1247731/exexutor+kit+ for+settling+an+estate.pdf/711b92a1-d415-42ad-a96b-4ec059201041, accessed on February 15, 2021.

Michaellas Gray, LL.B and John Budd, FCA. (2011). *The Canadian Guide to Will and Estate Planning*. Toronto: McGraw-Hill Education, Third Edition.

"The Unspoken Rite of Financial Passage." *Estateexec*. https://www.estateexec.com/Docs/Rite_of_Passage, accessed on February 15, 2021.

"Transferring. The Importance of Assistance—Estate Planning Guide for Manitoba Residents" (NATCAN Trust Company, 2013).

Van Caurrenberghe, Christine. (2017). *Wealth Planning Strategies for Canadians.* Toronto: Carswell.

Yih, Jim. (2020). "Estate Planning: Understanding Taxes & Probate Fees." *Retire Happy.* https://retirehappy.ca/estate-planning-understanding-taxes-and-probate- fees/ Last Update January 9, 2020.

Book Club
Discussion Questions

—

Hello, fellow book-clubbers. I hope you enjoyed reading *True to the End*

Here are a few questions for discussion.

1. The author was reluctant to take on the task of Executor. What do you see in her heart and mind that makes her uncomfortable with the mission?

2. Have you had the experience of serving as Executor? If yes, how was your experience similar or different from the one in this book?

3. Did you find the narrative and logistics associated with the role of Executor delineated in an "easy to digest" format, accessible even to a novice?

4. Did you learn about the business of executorship, the steps, commitment, responsibilities, hazards, stress?

5. Did the reflections and practicality outlined in the book invite you into the world of your own end-of-life decisions enough to take action?

6. The author is shocked at the discovery of Marilyn's addiction. Do you agree that one cannot know everything about close friends and family and that perhaps we aren't meant to know everything?

7. Family estrangement is one of the factors among the family dynamics in this memoir. Numerous studies on this topic show that estrangement is more common than we think. It's a painful experience, with people suffering through it choosing to be silent on their experience because they feel judged and misunderstood. Do you have thoughts to share on this?

8. Did the book impact your mood? If yes, in what way?

9. Did you find that the lighter sections provide relief from the seriousness and sadness of the story? What do they add to the narrative?

10. The author shares her humanity and vulnerability with an honest transparency throughout her journey. Was this helpful in developing credibility with the reader?

11. How did the character of the Executor come across—someone to like, dislike, pity, dismiss? Do you sympathize with her struggles?

12. As the story unfolds, you meet a varied "cast of characters" in a variety of circumstances. Did you find yourself able to relate to anyone specifically in this diverse group?

13. Did your opinion of the book change as you got further into it? What was your favourite and least favourite part?

14. Are there lingering questions from the book that you're noodling on and would like to ask if you could have dinner with the author?

Acknowledgements

I am indebted to every individual named in this book for travelling the Executor journey with me, lending exactly the hand I needed at every turn. You helped me achieve what I thought at the outset was impossible. I can't thank you enough.

I am forever grateful to family and friends who served as first readers, giving invaluable feedback on this work in progress: Kristianne Dechant, Peggy Gibson, Cathy Garvin, and Richard Turcotte. Thank you for your valuable perspectives and generous spirit. A special thank you also to my technology coach, Kristianne, even if you make fun of me at times.

I gladly acknowledge with gratitude the FriesenPress team, Emily, Andrea and Kerry in particular, who supported the development of this book in such spectacular fashion.

Thank you

Thank you

—

Thank you for reading *True to the End*. We would love to hear your thoughts about this book. Your review will be appreciated no matter how brief or long, humorous or serious. You may also wish to share your own journey or raise a question.

Please contact us for information about special discounts for bulk purchases.

www.germainedechant.ca

Lightning Source UK Ltd.
Milton Keynes UK
UKHW010806010721
386452UK00001B/53

9 781039 106932